BREWING THE
WORLD'S GREAT BEERS

BREWING THE WORLD'S GREAT BEERS

A STEP-BY-STEP GUIDE

DAVE MILLER

A Storey Publishing Book

Storey Communications, Inc.
Schoolhouse Road
Pownal, Vermont 05261

The mission of Storey Communications is to serve our customers
by publishing practical information that encourages personal independence
in harmony with the environment.

Cover design by Carol Jessop
Text design and production by Carol Jessop
Cover photographs by Nicholas Whitman
Illustrations by Kay Holmes Stafford and Carl F. Kirkpatrick
Indexed by Gail Damerow

Printed in the United States by R.R. Donnelley
Eighth Printing, April 1995

Library of Congress Cataloging-in-Publication Data

Miller, Dave G., 1945-
     Brewing the world's great beers : a step-by-step guide / Dave Miller.
p.   cm.
"A Storey Publishing book."
Includes bibliographical references and index.
ISBN 0-88266-776-9 (hc) — ISBN 0-88266-775-0 (pbk.)
1. Brewing—Amateurs' manuals.   I. Title.
TP570.M47   1992
641.8'73—dc20   91-50605
                                                                           CIP

Once again, to Diana

CONTENTS

ACKNOWLEDGMENTS

A special thank you to Roy Rudebusch of IMO Homebrew Supply and to John Sterling, both fellow members of the St. Louis Brews. Several of the illustrations in this book are based on photos of their home breweries.

Thanks also to Byron Burch of Great Fermentations in Santa Rosa, California, for permission to quote him in Chapter 5 and to reproduce the excellent Carbonation Chart found there.

And, finally, thanks to the American Homebrewers Association for permission to quote from their Mission Statement; and to Dee Roberson of the Home Wine and Beer Trade Association for her assistance with the Sources section at the end of the book.

INTRODUCTION

Welcome to the world of beer and brewing! This book was written to introduce you to the great beer styles of the world, and to lead you, step by step, to a mastery of the brewer's art. Whether you are a complete novice or already have some experience, you will find here a wealth of practical information on the equipment, ingredients, and techniques that are used by expert home brewers, and recipes that will give you beers with the authentic Old World flavor of the original types.

The emphasis here is on the word *practical*. If you are an advanced brewer and want to delve into the technology, chemistry, and biology of brewing, my earlier book, *The Complete Handbook of Home Brewing,* covers those subjects in some detail. This book focuses on the "what" rather than the "why." However, before we get into the "whats" of home brewing, there is one "why" question that has to be addressed. That is, why should I — or anyone for that matter — be so excited about making beer at home? What's this hobby all about?

Of all the great creations of civilization, few are more ancient or more important than beer. Archaeologists have found breweries in diggings from ancient Egypt and Sumeria — the oldest of all human cultures. From that time up to the present, beer has been one of the basic foodstuffs of the world, giving nourishment and pleasure to those who partake of it.

Not surprisingly, beer is as variable as bread. In preindustrial times, every town and village in Northern Europe had its own breweries and its own indigenous type or style of beer, and the great brewing nations there still boast a tremendous diversity of beer styles, each with its own devoted following.

As an immigrant nation, America once shared in this heritage. But economic and social factors gradually led to the ascendancy of a single beer style: the light, effervescent beverage that most of us now think of as beer. This almost universal sameness of style has turned beer into merely one of a number of competing commodities in the American beverage market. Beer no longer holds a central place in our cuisine or culture, as it does in Belgium, Great Britain, Germany, or Czechoslovakia.

But, remarkably, an interest in beer is reawakening among the American public. Beginning on the West Coast, in Oregon and California, a new generation of tiny local breweries (microbreweries) has sprung up, producing a variety of traditional beers that have found a small, but growing, niche in the American market.

The microbrewery movement was founded by home brewers who decided to make a profession out of their hobby. Most of them originally took up brewing as a challenge, an opportunity to use their hands and brains to create a unique and flavorful product, thereby recapturing both a piece of our cultural heritage and some of the tradition of personal craftsmanship that has gone by the boards in our postindustrial society. A well-made traditional beer is a profound pleasure; when you have created it yourself, doubly so.

This is not to say that home brewing was always so noble in its aims or its accomplishments. During Prohibition, it was a hasty, surreptitious craft whose sole guiding principle was that beer, no matter how wretched, is better than water. Having tasted some brews made by those methods, I am not sure I agree.

When Prohibition ended, home brewing was quickly and gladly abandoned. So great was the stigma upon it that forty years passed before a small number of determined and slightly unconventional Americans became interested in making their own beer. Fortunately, those early pioneers — Fred Eckhardt, Byron Burch, and Charlie Papazian, to name three of the most prominent — were also beer lovers, and in the 1970s all wrote books which empha-

sized quality and provided an impetus for home brewers to extend themselves, both in terms of their tastes and their techniques. When Papazian founded the American Homebrewers Association in 1979, he set the course of the movement in this country with his emphasis on "appreciation of the quality and variety of beer" (AHA Mission Statement). In the same year, Congress passed a law legalizing home brewing, and, a few years later, microbreweries began to spring up.

The mushrooming popularity of home brewing, plus the birth of a new microbrewing industry, has led to the development of new products and services aimed at this market. Malt extract syrups, long the mainstay of home brewers, have been improved to the point where beers brewed from them are often indistinguishable from those beers made with grain malt. Growers and merchants have recognized this new market and are now furnishing it with numerous varieties of high-quality hops. Small laboratories have sprung up to serve the growing demand for fresh, pure yeast cultures, which enable home brewers to duplicate the nuances of almost all the world's great beer styles.

Home brewing in America is now the most advanced in the world. Beers that win in national and regional competitions are fully comparable to the finest commercial examples of their type. Progressive retailers offer equipment and materials which are in every way equal, and often identical, to the products used by professional brewmasters. At the same time, home brewers have continued to find ingenious solutions to the technical problems posed by small-scale brewing. They have developed techniques which enable them to use their improved materials to the best advantage. With these resources, it is now possible to brew the great beers of the world at home, to your delight as well as that of your family and friends. The hard work of trial and error has already been done, and people who take up the hobby these days can quickly (often within a year) reach a standard of excellence which it took old-timers like myself a decade to achieve. I know; I have seen many members of my own club do it.

The problem remains that first year, when the home brewer has to learn the craft. The heart of this book is a plan I have developed to guide you through that process and maximize your chances of success. Following this outline, or course of study, if you prefer, you will be able to brew a good beer on your very first attempt, and then you will gradually, at your own pace, explore the sophisticated techniques that will expand your brewing horizons and capabilities.

The key to this plan is to match the style of beer and the materials you are working with to your level of experience. You will develop a body of brewing knowledge through experience, but you need to recognize your level of ability when choosing recipes and ingredients. Almost all beginners' recipes call for simple ingredients and methods, but they are often for types of beer which require more sophisticated techniques and/or materials (especially yeast) for first-class results.

Another problem with many beginners' recipes is that they are compromised by economic considerations. I believe this is a mistake. My goal is to help you succeed the first time out, even if that means paying a few extra dollars for your ingredients. Your beer will still be far less expensive than a comparable imported or microbrewed beer, and the satisfaction of making a good brew yourself is valuable in and of itself.

After reading this book, you will be making good beer from the very start. The only tradeoff required is a certain amount of flexibility on your part. I start with British ales because you can make some excellent ones using relatively simple procedures and equipment. You may have your heart set on duplicating Coors, but I would urge you to keep an open mind. Part of home brewing, after all, involves widening your horizons, and there are nearly a dozen styles of British ale, each one excellent in its own way. In addition, there are sound technical reasons for starting with ale. First of all, the higher fermentation temperatures are much easier to manage. Furthermore, as I have already hinted, yeast is the most important ingredient in determining a beer's flavor, and it can be the limiting factor. Even if you do everything else right, a poor yeast will always make a substandard product. Fortunately, there are several good British ale yeasts that are available in dry form. They are easy to use and are another reason why I strongly believe that you should start your trip through the world of brewing in Great Britain.

As you acquire more experience and equipment, you can move on to German and Belgian ales, and to the use of liquid-culture yeasts, which almost all experts regard as a vital component in these beers. You will also learn more sophisticated brewing techniques, which will give you even better results. Finally, you can move on to the Czech and German lager beers that require the most time and control to brew.

This step-by-step learning process does not mean, however, that you are locked into a fixed set of recipes or that, if your exploration of the world of beers leads you to a firm preference for the British styles, you are stuck with the relatively unsophisticated methods you first used to make them. The recipes are presented in such a way that it is easy to modify them to suit your taste, and to use more advanced materials (such as liquid yeasts) and techniques.

After you have explored the world of beer styles and learned some ad-

vanced methods, you will be ready to take the final step, which is to make your beers from grain malt as the commercial breweries do. Chapter 3 gives instructions and recipes for what I call partial-mash brewing, which requires relatively little equipment and allows you to learn the basic technique and acquire confidence in your ability to handle this sometimes intimidating process. Chapter 4 takes the final step into brewing entirely from grain — the last frontier and highest achievement for the home brewer.

There are some steps that, for one reason or another, do not fit neatly into this pattern. For example, home brewers differ in their attitude toward bottles and bottling. No one really likes it, but some people are more tolerant than others. One home brewer will start investing in draft equipment very early on, but another may put up with bottling for years. For this reason, an explanation of draft systems and advanced draft beer techniques is placed in a final chapter, along with a couple of other topics that you may want to explore at some point in your progress.

I wish you good luck, and hope you enjoy your brewing as much as I do. The only thing that's more fun than making a good beer is drinking it. Cheers!

GETTING STARTED

The best way to learn a new process is to actually do it, and I'm sure you are eager to begin. Before you make up a shopping list, though, please read this entire chapter. You will need to select a recipe before you buy ingredients. Also think about where you are going to do your brewing and fermenting and whether your circumstances may require some preparations. For example, if you live in a warm climate, you will need to find a cool space for fermentation.

THE BEGINNER'S EQUIPMENT KIT

Here is a list of the equipment needed for the simple brewing method outlined in this chapter. Sources are given in parentheses; items found in all kitchens (for example, a stove) are not included.

1. Large enamelware or stainless steel kettle with lid (discount, department, hardware, and restaurant

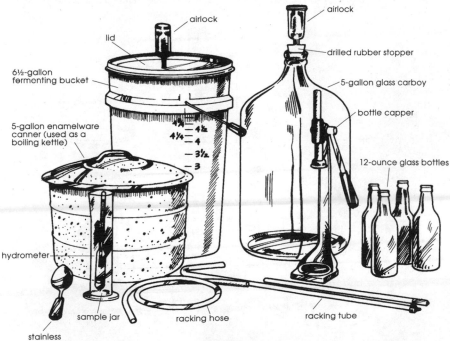

Figure 1–1. Basic homebrewing equipment.

supply stores). Minimum recommended capacity is 5 gallons. This kettle is used to boil brewing water and *wort* (the sugary solution of malt extract that will become beer).

2. Large stainless steel spoon (discount stores). For stirring the wort.

3. 6.5- to 10-gallon plastic fermenting bucket, preferably with a tight-fitting lid that will accept an airlock. The best place to get this is at a homebrew supply store; it *must* be food-grade plastic.

4. Racking tube (⅜ inch outside diameter — or o.d.) and 5 feet clear plastic hose, 5/16 i.d. (homebrew supply store). For siphoning beer from one container to another.

5. A 5-gallon glass carboy (homebrew supply store or bottled water

company). Plastic is not acceptable. This will be used as your secondary fermenter.

6. Three-piece airlock and No. 6.5 drilled white rubber stopper (homebrew supply store). The airlock fits in the stopper, which fits the mouth of the glass carboy. It keeps air from entering while allowing carbon dioxide to escape.

7. Carboy and bottle brushes (homebrew supply store). Used for cleaning.

8. Bottle capper (homebrew supply store). The best type has a stand for one-handed operation, and adjusts to different size bottles.

9. Hydrometer and sample jar (homebrew supply store). A hydrometer is used to measure the

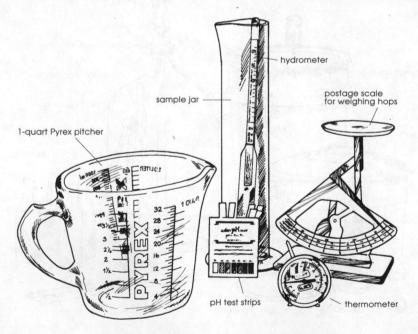

Figure 1–2. Basic measuring and testing material.

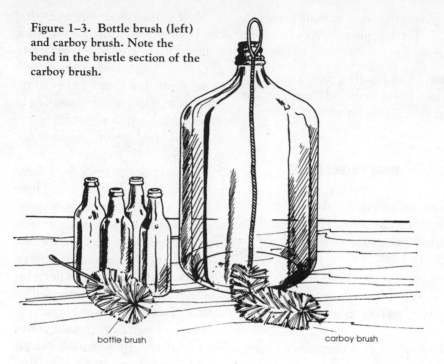

Figure 1–3. Bottle brush (left) and carboy brush. Note the bend in the bristle section of the carboy brush.

bottle brush   carboy brush

amount of sugar in the wort before fermentation begins. As fermentation goes on, the sugar is converted to alcohol. Comparing the hydrometer readings before and after fermentation allows you to calculate the alcohol content of your beer. Hydrometers are only accurate at 60°F.; yours should come with instructions and a table to allow you to correct for slight temperature variations.

10. Thermometer (homebrew supply store, lab supply store). Range should be 32° to 212°F. (0° to 100°C.). Dial thermometers are better because they react quickly. The best ones are marked off in one-degree increments and have an adjusting nut to allow calibra-

tion. Instructions for use are usually included.

11. Scale (homebrew supply store, or kitchen or office supply store). You need a small scale with a full range of 0 to 4 or 0 to 8 ounces, marked out in ¼-ounce divisions to accurately weigh out hops and specialty malts.

12. Bottles (bars, liquor stores, etc.). The best ones are the brown returnable "longnecks." One-way bottles and imported beer bottles are acceptable as long as they take a regular pry-off cap. Screw-thread types ("twist-or-pry") are not.

13. Fine-mesh nylon straining bag (homebrew supply store). Make sure it is very fine mesh. You put ingredients such as malt grains in this for steeping. Avoids messy straining.

14. Four 1-gallon jugs, preferably glass. For storing cold brewing water in your refrigerator.

MATERIALS

The following are the ingredients that actually go into your beer, plus other things that are "used up" in the process.

Malt Extract

The first step in commercial brewing is to convert the grain malt starches into sugar, a process known as *mashing*. The sweet liquid that is drawn off is called *wort*.

Malt extract is simply wort that has been concentrated to a thick syrup or, in the case of dry extract, to a powder. To make wort from malt extract, all that is needed is to reconstitute it in a suitable amount of water. Malt extract simplifies and speeds up the brewing process considerably.

Malt extract is made by a large number of manufacturers. Three colors are usually available: pale, amber, and dark. Some manufacturers make special extracts for specific purposes, such as weizenbier extract, which is made using a high percentage of wheat malt and is intended for making Bavarian wheat beers.

Hopped malt extracts (also called beer kits) are ordinary malt extract blended with hop extract. This theoretically eliminates the need to boil the wort, but your results will be better if you boil it anyway. I do not

Figure 1–4. Malt extracts are sold in various forms and packages. Left to right: dry malt extract powder; Northwestern malt extract syrup (packed in a plastic bag inside a box); and Alexander's malt extract syrup (canned, as are most brands of syrup).

recommend hopped extracts. You will get a better hop flavor, and better control over the bitterness of your beer, if you add your own hops. Also, the instructions on beer kits resemble old-style homebrew recipes — the results are a thin, cidery-flavored product.

Another problem you will run into with extracts is that flavor and color are not uniform from brand to brand. British pale malt extracts are made from pale ale malt, which produces a darker-colored wort than American pale malt extract. Others are made using special dark malts, which add flavor as well as color.

In general, I prefer to use unhopped pale malt extract and add color and flavor to my darker brews by employing specialty grains, such as crystal and dark malt, which are easy to work with. However, some of my recipes are based on specific amber or dark malt extracts made from a combination of malts to give *unique* flavors and aromas. Do not substitute brands in these cases.

The moral of the story is that you cannot switch brands haphazardly. Stick with the one you bought first until you gain a little experience; then you can do a controlled experiment (leaving everything else the same) to see what difference the extract will make.

Malt extract syrup and dry extract powder both have certain advantages, and my recipes use both. Dry malt extract is relatively easy to weigh out and measure. This makes it easy to adjust proportions and quantities, but dry malt extract absorbs water from the air and will harden into lumps if it is stored under humid conditions. In a damp climate, it should be stored in two layers of plastic, preferably with a silica gel bag.

Malt extract syrup avoids this problem, but it is sticky and hard to measure. In addition, it does not store well once the container has been opened: the syrup will darken and acquire a coarse, tangy flavor. This also happens, much more slowly, to unopened containers. Any type of malt extract should be used within three months of purchase, and you should try to get fresh products. Avoid cans that are bulging or dented, or bags of dry extract that have started to harden.

Water

Water is quite variable in its composition. It has a great influence on the mashing process, and advanced home brewers have to pay close attention to the mineral content of their water. When brewing from malt extract, the situation is much simpler. Basically, there are two things you have to worry about with municipal water — chlorine and bacteria.

Chlorine is important because it can harm beer flavor. Almost all municipal water supplies are chlorinated, and such water should be boiled for 15 minutes before you brew with it. Remember that all the water must be boiled — not only what you use for making up your wort, but any water you add later on. I give instructions for this in my Basic Method, which begins on page 15.

An alternative to boiling is carbon filtration, which is gaining in popularity. Many homes now have these filters installed in the drinking-water line, and they are quite effective in removing chlorine. However, carbon filters must be well maintained, because they form a fertile breeding ground for bacteria — the very thing the chlorine is supposed to eliminate. Unless your carbon filter includes a bacteriostatic element, or a sterile filter to trap bacteria, I would recommend boiling your brewing water to eliminate this worry. Bacteria found in water supplies can spoil wort, leaving a cooked-cabbage odor in the finished beer.

Water from private wells is not usually chlorinated, but bacteria are a real possibility and such water must be boiled before use. Another problem is that well water often contains iron and manganese. If your well water has this problem, you already know it because the metallic taste is obvious. The only practical remedy for a home brewer is to demineralize your brewing water using one of the deionizing filters available from lab supply stores. Once again, boiling is recommended to ensure that it is bacteria-free after filtration.

Other alternatives to well water are to obtain municipal water from a nearby community or to buy bottled water. I strongly recommend the former: there are currently no federal standards for bottled water, and its quality is therefore variable and hard to guarantee.

Hops

The hops used in brewing are the cones (flowers) of the female hop plant. These cones contain soft resins called *alpha acids* that impart bitterness to beer. They also contain oils made up of aromatic compounds, which impart the hop flavor and aroma characteristic of many styles of beer.

Hop cones may be dried and compressed, in which case they are called *whole hops* or *leaf hops*. If they are ground into a powder and pressed into pellets they are called *pelletized hops*. Pellets are far less bulky than whole hops and, if properly packaged, are less vulnerable to deterioration during storage. Both forms make excellent beers, but you should choose your hops for their quality and freshness rather than for the form in which you find them. If you have a choice, pellets are easier to work with and are more suitable for beginning brewers.

Hops are among the most delicate of all brewing ingredients. They can deteriorate in a matter of weeks if they are not stored and handled properly. Hop pellets can be stored at room temperature if they are packaged in a "vapor barrier" foil bag

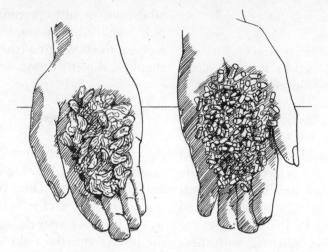

Figure 1–5. Whole hops (left) and pelletized hops (right).

filled with nitrogen. Whole hops (leaf hops) and pellets not sealed under nitrogen must be kept as cold as possible. You should only buy such hops from a supplier who keeps them refrigerated or frozen. Once you buy them, store them in the freezer.

There are dozens of hop varieties available, and they are broadly classified into two types. *Noble hops* are low in bitterness but have a pleasant aroma and flavor. *High-alpha hops* have high bitterness but (usually) a less pleasant aroma. High-alpha hops are more economical because you use less per batch, but the flavor often suffers, especially with the lighter, more delicate styles of beer.

Older recipes usually called for hops to be measured in ounces. This method led to inconsistent results, so today's homebrew recipes give hop rates in *alpha acid units* (AAUs), which are also known as *homebrew*

bittering units. Though more complex, the new measurement system gives consistent results from batch to batch, enabling the home brewer to control bitterness levels in his or her beer. It is calculated as follows:

Alpha Acid Units (AAUs) =
alpha acid percentage
✕ weight in ounces

Hops are analyzed and the bitter resin (alpha acid) content is given on the package as a percentage of total weight. Typical figures for the Hallertau variety, for example, are 3.5 to 4.5 percent. The Hallertaus I bought last year are 3.9 percent alpha acid. Each ounce of these hops contains 3.9 Alpha Acid Units. If I had a recipe calling for 8 AAUs of hops, I would need 2.05 ounces of Hallertau to make up this amount (8 ÷ 3.9 = 2.05 approximately). In practice, I would round this off to 2 ounces, which is close enough.

Hop weight (in ounces) =
AAUs required by recipe ÷ alpha acid content (listed on package)

Suppose I want to make the same recipe next year, but the hops I have available are Perle, with an alpha content of 6.5 percent. Doing the same calculation, I find that 8 divided by 6.5 is 1.23, which I would round off to 1.25. Thus to get the same level of bitterness with these more potent hops, I would use only 1¼ ounces.

I hope this exercise shows you why the AAU system has become almost universal in home brewing. Since the bittering power (alpha acid content) of various hop types can vary so dramatically — from 2.5

all the way up to 13 percent — the only way I can give you a reliable recipe is to ask you to do the kind of simple arithmetic shown above.

Yeast

As mentioned in the introduction, yeast is a critical brewing ingredient. To make a good beer you need both the right *type* of yeast (in other words, ale yeast for ales, lager yeast for lagers) and the right *strain* of yeast — one that is suitable for the style of beer you want to brew. All yeasts are not created equal.

By a long chalk, the most convenient form of yeast for brewers to use is the dry granules sold in homebrew supply stores in small foil packs. All you need to do is cut open the pack-

Figure 1–6. Forms of yeast. Brewer's choice liquid culture in foil packet (left); dried yeast in foil packet (right).

age, empty it into a cup of warm water, and let it sit for about 10 minutes to allow the little yeast cells to rehydrate. Just that quickly, you've got a "slurry" ready to pitch into your wort.

There are many brands of dried yeast, but only a few have proven to be "up to snuff" in terms of their performance. I strongly recommend that you stick to the brands given in the recipes at the end of this chapter. Also, remember that dry yeast is a one-shot proposition — you use a new packet for every batch. Yeast packets should be stored in the refrigerator and should not be shipped during the summer. Heat kills yeast, even dried yeast. Finally, buy your yeast fresh; ask your supplier when it was manufactured. Dry yeast slowly loses its viability.

Specialty Grains

These malt grains are made by various special processes which allow them to be used without mashing. You need only steep them in your brewing water for half an hour to release their flavor and color into your wort.

Crystal malt is probably the most widely used specialty grain. It imparts a reddish amber color and a sweet caramel flavor. Domestic crystal malt is available in a range of colors from 10 to 120 degrees Lovibond. Brewers use the Lovibond scale to measure the color of malt, wort, and beer: the higher the number, the darker the product. The dark grades of crystal malt have a sharp, roasted flavor. Lighter grades have a smooth, rich taste. Grades are not interchangeable.

There are also several types of dark roasted grains available to add color and flavor to dark beers. Chocolate malt is deep brown and imparts a rich, toasty flavor. Roasted barley has a sharper burnt taste, typical of stouts and porters. Domestic black malt is very dark in color, but it has a mild, smooth flavor and is used in dark beers when the distinct strong flavors of the other roasted grains are not desired.

All specialty grains should be stored in plastic bags to keep moisture out. Refrigeration is not necessary, but they do lose flavor over time and should be purchased in small quantities — 1 or 2 pounds at a time — because a little will go a long way.

Sugars

These materials are used as additional sources of fuel (for the fermentation process) and alcohol (for the final product). Overuse of sugar always leads to a thin, cidery taste in the finished beer. I advise using sugars only for specific purposes: for example, a small dose of corn sugar (dextrose) must be added when homebrew is bottled. This "priming" sugar starts a second fermentation that carbonates the beer. Corn sugar is available in all homebrew supply stores and is preferred for priming because it gives a faster, cleaner fermentation. Dark sugars, including molasses, impart unique flavors and are sometimes called for in traditional ale recipes.

Some sugars and syrups are made specifically for brewing from corn, rice, or barley, and intended as substitutes for the unmalted grain used by commercial brewers. Some of these products are quite satisfactory; others are not. Buy only from a reputable, knowledgeable supplier.

Miscellaneous Brewing Materials

Some brewers use preservatives, such as ascorbic acid or sodium metabisulfite, to try to enhance the keeping quality of their beers. Recent research has turned opinion against them, but you will find them mentioned in many older recipes. I believe they should be avoided.

Yeast nutrients (sometimes called yeast energizers or yeast food) are another class of product that was often called for in old recipes. These compounds typically contain ammonium phosphate as well as B-complex vitamins, such as biotin, which yeast needs to ferment. Yeast nutrients are marketed under various brand names and are available at homebrewing supply stores.

In general, any beer containing at least 1 pound of malt extract (or grain malt) per gallon will have an adequate supply of everything the yeast needs. But very light beers may benefit from yeast nutrients.

Cleaning and sanitizing materials are a vital part of any brewer's inventory. Trisodium phosphate (TSP), available at paint stores, is good for heavy-duty cleaning; ordinary dishwashing liquids work fine for lighter jobs. Unscented liquid chlorine bleach is the only sanitizing agent a home brewer needs. Other effective products, such as a TSP-and-chlorine combination and B-Brite, another cleaner-sanitizer, are available at homebrew supply shops. Like any household chemicals, these agents may be harmful to septic systems.

KEEPING RECORDS

Before brewing your first batch of beer, make up and use some sort of notebook. This can take any form, from a simple legal pad to a directory on the hard disk of your personal computer. Use it to record your brewing activities in as much detail as possible. At a minimum, record the exact recipe you use, plus the dates, times, procedures, etc., of every step in the process. Specific gravity and temperature readings are very important, as are taster's notes on the finished product.

Keeping records will allow you to learn from each brewing session, to improve upon your successes, and to avoid repeating your mistakes. It is no exaggeration to say that the speed of a brewer's progress is proportional to the time he or she puts into keeping records.

THE BASIC METHOD

Brewing appears complicated to beginners, but actually it is a simple process that breaks down into a sequence of easy steps. First, wort is made by steeping specialty grains in hot water and then dissolving the malt extract. Then the wort is boiled with the hops. After this, the wort is cooled, aerated, and pitched with a slurry of active brewer's yeast. The yeast then ferments the wort, converting its sugars into alcohol and carbon dioxide. Finally, the beer is bottled and aged to bring it to its best flavor. After that, there is nothing left but to enjoy it!

Making the Wort

A day or two before brewing, prepare 4 gallons of cold water. First boil it for at least 15 minutes, then let it cool, covered. Clean and sanitize four 1-gallon jugs by carefully washing them, then add 2 tablespoons of chlorine bleach to one of the jugs and fill it with water. Allow the bleach solution to stand 10 minutes in each jug before pouring it into the next one. Rinse the jugs thoroughly three times, then fill with the cool boiled water. Store the jugs in the refrigerator or in an ice-water bath.

On brewing day, check your recipe to see if specialty malts are called for. If so, you must weigh them out and crush them. It is best to use a grain mill for this, and most homebrew supply stores have one for their

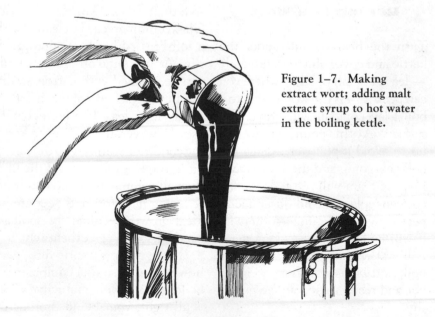

Figure 1–7. Making extract wort; adding malt extract syrup to hot water in the boiling kettle.

customers to use. If not, you can do the job with a rolling pin or champagne bottle on a hard, flat surface. Put the crushed grains in your nylon mesh bag.

Draw 2 gallons of hot tap water into your 5-gallon kettle. Turn the heat on full, cover, and bring to a boil. Turn off the heat and let the water stand, uncovered, until the temperature falls to 160°F. Put the grain bag in the kettle and let the grain steep for half an hour, stirring occasionally. Remove the bag before proceeding. Add the malt extract and stir well to dissolve. If using malt extract syrup, rinse the container by pouring in some of your hot wort and swishing it around — otherwise quite a bit of the syrup will cling to the walls of the container and be wasted.

Boiling the Wort

Turn the heat on full under the kettle and cover almost completely — leave a small opening where you can peek in. As the wort comes to a boil, a layer of foam will form on the surface. At this point, remove the lid to avoid a boilover. Once the boil gets going and the wort is rolling, the foam will settle down and you can replace the lid. Just remember to leave an opening — otherwise it will boil over and make a mess. Follow the recipe as to length of boil, and have your hops weighed out and ready to add at the proper time.

Bittering hops are usually added at one or two points during the boil, anywhere from 20 to 60 minutes before the end. Aroma or finishing hops are usually added 5 or 10 minutes before the end of the boil, or occasionally at the very end. In any case, for consistent results it is important to follow the schedule given in the recipe.

Sanitation

During the boil, clean your fermenter with detergent and sanitize it with a chlorine solution: 2 tablespoons of chlorine bleach per gallon of water (remember to use only unscented bleach). As an alternative you can clean and sanitize in a single step using the special chlorinated TSP available from homebrew shops.

Never use anything more abrasive than a sponge to clean plastic. Glass containers can be cleaned with a soft-bristled brush of appropriate size. Airlocks and other small items can be cleaned with cotton swabs. Plastic hoses and tubing must be soaked for at least 10 minutes before use. However, the real key to keeping conditions sanitary is to clean up or, in the case of hoses and the like, soak all equipment immediately after using it. Wort and beer are an ideal growth medium for spoilage bacteria, so don't give them a chance.

There is some controversy over how best to rinse your equipment. I believe that, if your municipal water is all right, you should thoroughly

Figure 1–8. Rinsing out a carboy in the kitchen sink using a sprayer.

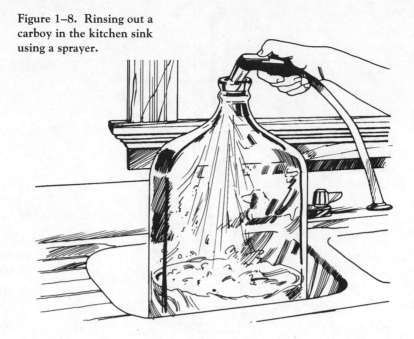

rinse all equipment after cleaning and sanitizing. Then it is ready to be used again or to be drained dry. However, if your tap water is questionable, rinse with a brief wash or soak in a highly dilute chlorine solution (2 tablespoons of bleach per 5 gallons water). At this level, the chlorine will not affect the flavor of your beer, but it will knock out any stray bacteria in your tap water.

How do you know if your water is OK? Call your local water company and ask them for the bacteria count of the water. It should be zero.

Cooling the Wort and Pitching the Yeast

After boiling is completed, let the wort stand in the kettle under cover for 10 minutes. Then add 2 gallons of cold water you prepared the day before. Pour the wort into your clean sanitized fermenter. (Note: If you used whole hops in the boil, pour the wort through a clean, sanitized, stainless steel strainer.) Then add more cold water to bring the level up to 5 gallons. This will lower the temperature of the wort considerably, but it will still be too hot to pitch with yeast. Cover the fermenter and stand it in a bathtub or other large container of cold water— the colder the better. Stir the wort every 20 minutes or so and check the temperature. When it falls to 65°F., you are ready to pitch.

Either just before or after pitching, take a specific gravity reading of your wort using the hydrometer. Follow the instructions that came

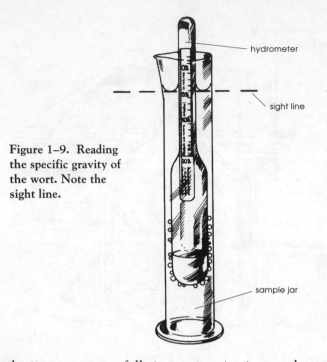

Figure 1–9. Reading the specific gravity of the wort. Note the sight line.

with the instrument carefully in order to get an accurate reading. Remember that the hydrometer, like the spoon and everything else, must be clean and sanitized before it comes in contact with the wort.

During cooling, boil a cup of water and then cool it to 100°F. If you are in a hurry, you can force-cool the water by standing a Pyrex measuring cup in a sink full of cold water. When the water has reached the correct temperature, remove it from the cooling bath and add the yeast. Allow to stand at least 10 minutes, but not more than 30, before pitching. Usually the timing works out if you rehydrate the yeast, as described here, when the wort is only a few degrees above pitching temperature.

After pitching the yeast, you must aerate the wort thoroughly in order to give it a good start. Yeast needs oxygen to grow. If your fermenter can be tightly closed, do so, and then shake it vigorously for at least 10 minutes. If you cannot shake for that long, shake it for 2 minutes, let it sit for an hour, then shake again; repeat this four times. If shaking is out of the question, use a sanitized stainless steel spoon to stir the wort vigorously for 5 minutes, and repeat this four more times.

Fermentation

After pitching and aerating your wort, put it in a cool spot (62° to 68°F.), attach an airlock, and leave it alone. By observing the airlock, you will be able to track the progress of fermentation.

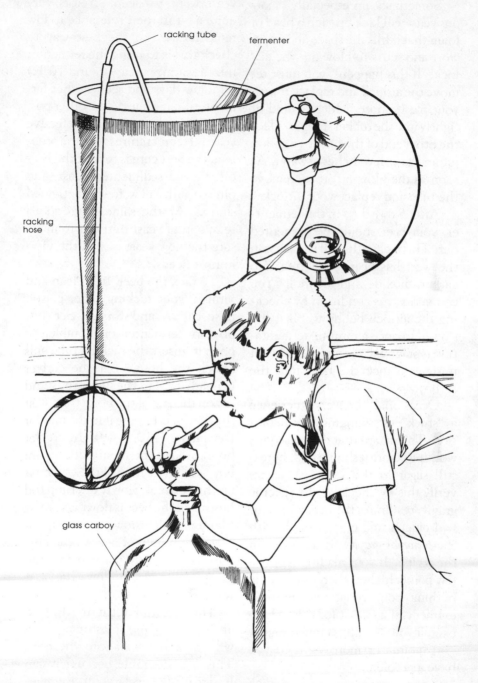

racking tube

fermenter

racking
hose

glass carboy

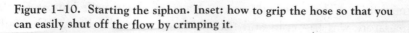

Figure 1–10. Starting the siphon. Inset: how to grip the hose so that you can easily shut off the flow by crimping it.

Sometimes, an especially vigorous yeast will kick up such a head of foam that it fills the space above the wort and starts to blow out the airlock. If this happens, you must remove the airlock and replace it with your plastic hose, which should fit tightly into the rubber stopper. Place the other end of the hose in a gallon jug and add a few inches of water. As soon as the blow-off stops, remove the tube and replace your airlock.

After 5 to 7 days in the fermenter, your beer should be fermented out. This means that all the sugar in the wort has been converted into carbon dioxide and alcohol. You can verify this condition by checking the airlock bubbling. If it has slowed to once a minute, fermentation is practically complete. Then it is time to rack the beer into the carboy.

Occasionally brewers experience a "stuck" or "hanging" fermentation. This means that the yeast quits working before it should and there is still sugar in the wort. You can verify this by checking the specific gravity reading of the beer with your hydrometer and comparing it with the *terminal gravity* figure given in the recipe. If your reading is only a few points higher, there is probably nothing wrong; variations in the malt extract can account for this. However, if your reading is much higher — 6 points or more — then you have a problem.

There are two reasons for a stuck fermentation. The first is that the temperature was too cold and the yeast went to sleep. Yeasts vary quite a bit in their tolerance to low temperatures, so the best way to check this is to bring the fermenter into a warmer area (around 70°F.) for a few days and see whether fermentation resumes. The other possibility is malnourished or defective yeast. If temperature is not the problem, the best cure is to rack the beer off the old sedimented yeast, and pitch it with a new, freshly activated slurry. At the same time, add a teaspoon of yeast nutrient to make sure the new yeast has all the vitamins it needs.

To rack the beer, first clean and sanitize your racking tube, plastic hose, carboy, and stopper. Set your primary fermenter on a tabletop, open it, insert the racking tube and attach the hose. Set the carboy beneath it. Start the siphon by sucking on the end of the hose, then stop the flow by crimping it in the middle (see Figure 1–10, p. 19). Insert the hose through the mouth of the carboy, and lower it until the end rests on the bottom. Slowly uncrimp the hose until the beer is flowing gently. Maintain a slow flow rate until there is about an inch of beer in the bottom. At this point you can uncrimp completely and let it flow as fast as it wants.

The reason for restricting the flow at first is to avoid splashing, which will incorporate air into the beer. This is undesirable because it can lead to off-flavors later on. Remember, oxygen or air is almost always bad for wort and beer. The only

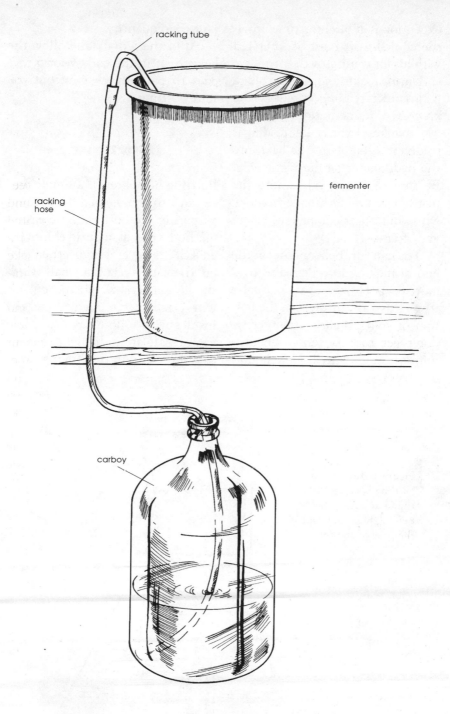

racking tube

racking
hose

fermenter

carboy

Figure 1–11. Racking the fermented beer into the carboy.

exception is at pitching time, when the cooled wort must be saturated with air for yeast growth.

During racking you should take a hydrometer reading to check the progress of fermentation. The best way to take a hydrometer reading is to divert a sample of the beer into the hydrometer jar during racking. Be sure to clean and sanitize the instrument and its sample jar along with your other equipment, before and after use.

You can tilt the fermenter at the end of racking in order to recover more beer. However, you must also try to leave all the dregs in the bottom of your primary fermenter, so don't get too concerned about a minor loss. Quality is more impor-tant than quantity.

Affix the airlock and allow the beer to sit in the carboy for 5 to 7 days to partially clear before you start bottling.

Bottling

Bottling homebrew is a simple pro-cedure; the only real difficulty is in preparing the bottles. The easiest method is to soak them in chlorinat-ed TSP for several hours, then peel off the labels using a small wind-shield scraper. Scrub the outside with a nylon scouring pad and the insides with a bottle brush. Hold each bottle up to the light to make sure there is nothing clinging to the

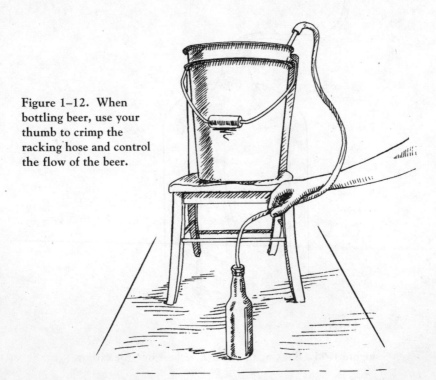

Figure 1–12. When bottling beer, use your thumb to crimp the racking hose and control the flow of the beer.

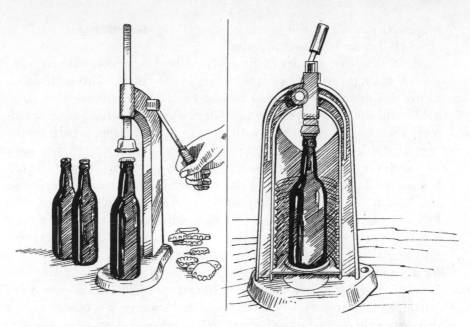

Figure 1–13. Two common types of bottle cappers.

bottom or sides. Rinse three times in warm water. At this point the bottles are clean and ready for the final sanitizing step, which should be done shortly before filling them.

To sanitize the bottles, either run them through a dishwasher using plain water (no detergent) and ending with the "heat dry" cycle or soak them in a dilute chlorine solution (2 tablespoons chlorine per 5 gallons water) and let them drain dry upside down.

Bottle-cleaning is tiresome, but once your bottles are cleaned and delabeled, you can maintain them in good condition by rinsing them out thoroughly as soon as they become empty and storing them upside down. Then you need only repeat the final sanitizing step before refilling.

You need about fifty-four 12-ounce bottles for 5 gallons of beer. When the bottles are ready, make up a syrup by adding your priming sugar (specified in the recipe) to 2 cups of boiling water. Stir to dissolve. Then clean and sanitize your racking tube, hose, and a plastic bucket. Rack the beer out of the carboy into the bucket and add the priming sugar syrup. Try not to splash, but stir as vigorously as you can with your racking tube for 2 minutes to disperse the syrup. Then stand the bucket on a high shelf or on top of a refrigerator. Place the bottles on a table or counter below. Start the siphon, but immediately crimp the hose when the brew is about 12 inches from the bottom. Put the hose in the first bottle, and partially uncrimp the hose, but keep a grip on it. When the bottle is almost full, raise the hose to near the level of the beer and let it flow slowly, raising it as the beer rises. Using this method, you should be able to fill the bottle to the proper level (½ inch below the top) with very little splashing. Then stop the flow and move on to the next bottle. Repeat until you are finished. You will have to fill the last few bottles by hand, using a pitcher.

Next, put the caps loosely on the tops of the bottles and let them sit for 15 minutes or so while you do some cleaning up. This allows the bottle fermentation to start and drives some air out of the headspace. Cap the bottles, rinse them, and, when dry, store them upright in their cases for a week at 60° to 65°F., then for another 3 weeks in a cooler spot (50°F., if possible) before decanting and drinking.

Serving

Homebrew is carbonated by fermenting in the bottle. This is an excellent and inexpensive method, but it does leave a thin layer of yeast sediment in the bottom of each bottle. To avoid a yeasty taste, you must carefully pour off (decant) the entire bottle into a glass before drinking. Furthermore, you must take care when transporting homebrew not to agitate the bottles or let them tip over.

If you follow these rules, your homebrewed ale will be reasonably clear. However, you cannot expect it to be crystal clear like a commercial bottled beer, since it has not been filtered or treated with clarifying agents. Remember that the epitome of ale is the unfiltered "real ale" that is conditioned (carbonated) right in the cask; discriminating Brit-

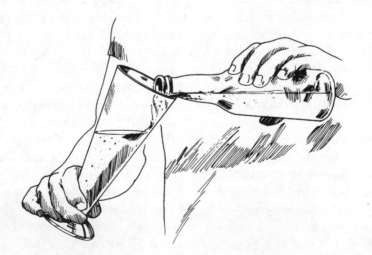

Figure 1–14. Decanting bottled home brew.

ons seek out these brews and scorn the clear, filtered types. Clarity, in my opinion, is vastly overrated. However, if you want to make a sparkling clear beer, there are a number of methods for doing so, which are discussed in the following chapters.

Meanwhile, enjoy your authentic, bottle-conditioned beer. Remember that it is not lager and should be served at 50° to 60°F., the range within which its flavor will be at its fullest. Avoid refrigerating, except if necessary for a brief cool-down just before serving. Ice-cold liquids numb the taste buds, and the point of a good ale is to satisfy the palate, not merely quench the thirst.

NOTES ON THE RECIPES

Any published homebrew recipe should be regarded as a starting point. Once you try it, you will probably want to adjust it to suit your own taste. Hop rates, malt extract, and specialty malts all can be varied to get the balance of flavors that you feel is appropriate.

The yeasts specified have generally given good results in practical trials. Each has its own flavor characteristics. If your results are unsatisfactory, a bad batch of any yeast may be responsible, so try another brand, but follow the same recipe and methods. That way you will know that any difference is really due to the yeast.

If you are not sure whether the unsatisfactory taste is due to yeast or not, your best bet is to take a bottle to your local homebrew shop or club for an evaluation. Experienced home brewers can almost always tell whether a problem arises from a bad fermentation or was caused by some other factor.

All the recipes for British ale that follow are based on the basic method. Probably the hardest part of the process is deciding which beer to brew. The brief descriptions below should help you make a choice, but they are no substitute for your own research (i.e., critical, attentive drinking).

Pale ale (known in draft form as bitter) is the national drink of Great Britain. It is amber in color, malty, with medium to high bitterness and, usually, a strong fresh hop aroma. Good examples are Bass and Young's Ram Rod.

Light ale is a bottled beer with less of everything — color, malt flavor, and aroma — than pale ale. Commercial examples are difficult to find in North America.

Mild ale and **brown ale** are basically the draft and bottled versions of the same type of beer. They are sweeter and less bitter than pale ale, with little hop aroma. Newcastle Brown is the best-known example, but it is not really typical: most browns are darker and have a distinct caramel note.

Scotch ale is similar to brown, but stronger and sweeter. They may be anywhere from light brown to almost black in color. MacEwan's is a good example of this style.

Old ale is darker than Scotch ale, quite strong, with a strong rum-like flavor that comes from a generous use of molasses. Old Peculier is a well-known example.

Porter was almost extinct commercially until it was revived by the microbreweries in this country. The toughest thing about creating a porter is that nobody really knows how it differs from stout. My recipe is basically a smoother version of dry stout.

The paradigm of **dry stout** is Guinness. No description can substitute for a taste of this remarkable brew.

Imperial stout is basically a very high-alcohol sweet stout, originally made for the czars of Old Russia. This style has lately been revived by Samuel Smith and several other brewers.

Barley wine is another high-alcohol ale, very sweet but also well-hopped, at least 8 percent alcohol by volume. Young's Old Nick is a good example, but most others are even stronger. Like Imperial Stout, this brew should be drunk at home, sitting in a comfortable chair.

RECIPES

All recipes yield approximately 5 gallons (U.S.) of beer.

PALE ALE (BITTER)

Malt extract: 3.3 lbs. British pale syrup, unhopped; plus 2 lbs. British pale dry, unhopped

Specialty grain: 8 oz. 40° L. (degrees Lovibond — see discussion on page 13) crystal malt

Bittering hops: 11 AAUs — Fuggles, Goldings, or Northern Brewer

Finishing hops: 1.5 oz. Goldings

Yeast: two 7-gram packets Munton & Fison or 1 packet Edme or Whitbread

Priming sugar: ½ cup corn sugar

Follow the Basic Method.

Brewer's Specifics

Original gravity of the wort: 1.042

Total time of boil: 45 minutes

Add the bittering hops at the beginning of the boil.

Add the finishing hops at the end of the boil.

Terminal gravity at the end of fermentation: 1.007–1.011.

LIGHT ALE

Malt extract: 3.3 lbs. British pale syrup, unhopped; plus 1 lb. British pale dry, unhopped

Specialty grain: 4 oz. 20°L. crystal malt

Bittering hops: 7 AAUs — Fuggles, Goldings, or Northern Brewer

Finishing hops: 1 oz. Goldings

Yeast: two 7-gram packets Munton & Fison or 1 packet Edme or Whitbread

Yeast nutrient: 1 teaspoon

Priming sugar: ½ cup corn sugar

Follow the Basic Method.

Brewer's Specifics

Original gravity: 1.033

Total time of boil: 45 minutes

Add the bittering hops at the beginning of the boil.

Add the finishing hops at the end of the boil.

Terminal gravity: 1.004–1.008.

BROWN ALE (MILD)

Malt extract: 3.3 lbs. British pale syrup, unhopped; plus 1 lb. British pale dry, unhopped
Specialty grains: 8 oz. 40°L. crystal malt; plus 4 oz. chocolate malt
Sugar: 1 lb. dark brown sugar (add to wort)
Bittering hops: 6 AAUs — Fuggles, Goldings, or Northern Brewer
Finishing hops: none
Yeast: two 7-gram packets Munton & Fison or 1 packet Edme or Whitbread
Yeast nutrient: 1 teaspoon
Priming sugar: ½ cup corn sugar

Follow the Basic Method.

Brewer's Specifics

Original gravity: 1.042
Total time of boil: 45 minutes
Add the bittering hops at the beginning of the boil.
Terminal gravity: 1.006–1.010.

SCOTCH ALE

Malt extract: 6.6 lbs. British pale syrup, unhopped
Specialty grains: 1 lb. 40°L. crystal malt; plus 4 oz. chocolate malt
Sugar: 1 lb. dark brown sugar (add to wort)
Bittering hops: 8 AAUs — Fuggles, Goldings, or Northern Brewer
Finishing hops: none
Yeast: two 7-gram packets Munton & Fison or 1 packet Edme or Whitbread
Sugar for priming: ½ cup corn sugar

Follow the Basic Method.

Brewer's Specifics

Original gravity: 1.055
Total time of boil: 45 minutes
Add the bittering hops at the beginning of the boil.
Terminal gravity: 1.010–1.016.

OLD ALE

Malt extract: 6.6 lbs. British pale syrup, unhopped
Specialty grains: 1 lb. 60°L. crystal malt; plus 8 oz. chocolate malt
Sugar: 24 oz. light molasses (add to wort)
Bittering hops: 9 AAUs — Fuggles, Goldings, or Northern Brewer
Finishing hops: none
Yeast: two 7-gram packets Munton & Fison or 1 packet Edme or Whitbread
Priming sugar: ½ cup corn sugar

Follow the Basic Method.

Brewer's Specifics

Original gravity: 1.060
Total time of boil: 45 minutes
Add the bittering hops at the beginning of the boil.
Terminal gravity: 1.012–1.016.

PORTER

Malt extract: 3.3 lbs. British pale syrup, unhopped; plus 2 lbs. British pale
    dry, unhopped
Specialty grain: 8 oz. roasted barley
Bittering hops: 10 AAUs — Northern Brewer or other high-alpha hops
Finishing hops: none
Yeast: two 7-gram packets Munton & Fison or 1 packet Edme or Whitbread
Priming sugar: ½ cup corn sugar

Follow the Basic Method.

Brewer's Specifics

Original gravity: 1.042
Total time of boil: 45 minutes
Add the bittering hops at the beginning of the boil.
Terminal gravity: 1.007–1.011.

DRY STOUT

Malt extract: 3.3 lbs. British pale syrup, unhopped; plus 2.5 lbs. British pale dry, unhopped

Specialty grain: 1 lb. roasted barley

Bittering hops: 12 AAUs — Northern Brewer or other high-alpha hops

Finishing hops: none

Yeast: two 7-gram packets Munton & Fison or 1 packet Edme or Whitbread

Priming sugar: ½ cup corn sugar

Follow the Basic Method.

Brewer's Specifics

Original gravity: 1.048

Total time of boil: 45 minutes

Add the bittering hops at the beginning of the boil.

Terminal gravity: 1.010–1.014.

IMPERIAL STOUT

Malt extract: 6.6 lbs. British dark syrup, unhopped; plus 3 lbs. British pale dry, unhopped

Specialty grains: 1 lb. 60°L. crystal malt; plus 4 oz. roasted barley; plus 4 oz. chocolate malt

Sugar: 1 lb. dark brown sugar (add to wort)

Bittering hops: 12 AAUs — Northern Brewer or other high-alpha hops

Finishing hops: none

Yeast: two 7-gram packets Munton & Fison or 1 packet Edme or Whitbread

Priming sugar: ½ cup corn sugar

Follow the Basic method, except that you should use 3 gallons of water to make up the wort. Add only 2 gallons of cold water to the kettle at the end of the boil.

Brewer's Specifics

Original gravity: 1.082

Total time of boil: 1 hour

Add the bittering hops at the beginning of the boil.

Terminal gravity: 1.014–1.020.

SWEET STOUT

Malt extract: 3.3 lbs. British pale syrup, unhopped; plus 2 lbs. British pale
  dry, unhopped
Specialty grains: 8 oz. 60°L. crystal malt; plus 8 oz. roasted barley
Bittering hops: 8 AAUs — Northern Brewer or other high-alpha hops
Finishing hops: none
Yeast: two 7-gram packets Munton & Fison or 1 packet Edme or Whitbread
Yeast nutrient: 1 teaspoon
Priming sugar: ½ cup corn sugar

Follow the Basic Method.

Brewer's Specifics

Original gravity: 1.045
Total time of boil: 45 minutes
Add the bittering hops at the beginning of the boil.
Terminal gravity: 1.008–1.011.

BARLEY WINE

Malt extract: 6.6 lbs. British pale syrup, unhopped; plus 3 lbs. British pale
  dry, unhopped
Specialty grain: 1 lb. 40°L. crystal malt
Sugar: 1.5 lbs. light brown or raw sugar (add to wort)
Bittering hops: 18 AAUs — Northern Brewer or other high-alpha hops
Finishing hops: none
Yeast: two 7-gram packets Munton & Fison or 1 packet Edme or Whitbread
Priming sugar: ½ cup corn sugar

*Follow the Basic Method, except that you should use 3 gallons of water to
make up the wort. Add only 2 gallons of cold water to the kettle at the
end of the boil.*

Brewer's Specifics

Original gravity: 1.086
Total time of boil: 1 hour
Add the bittering hops at the beginning of the boil.
Terminal gravity: 1.014–1.020.

STEPS TO BETTER BREWING WITH MALT EXTRACT

Now that you have learned the basic brewing method and used it to make some good ale, you are undoubtedly feeling a lot more confident. You are ready to learn more about brewing technique and try your hand at some new styles of beer.

This chapter outlines a series of steps that will enable you to brew any type of beer from malt extract. The most important is the use of pure yeast cultures, so that comes first, but the others are also worthwhile. Remember that everything you will learn here can be applied to the British ale recipes given in the previous chapter. For example, there are a number of strains of British ale yeast available in pure cultures, and these may be substituted for the dry yeasts to give even better results. For specific recommendations on which strains to use with which styles

of beer, consult the British ale recipes in Chapter 3.

The last of these steps is lager fermentation. The two main differences between lager and ale are in the yeast and fermentation method involved. There is no satisfactory lager yeast available in dry form, and there may never be. This means that you have to learn how to handle liquid yeasts if you want to make this type of beer. Furthermore, the other steps outlined here — wort cooling and trub separation, for example — are more important with lager than ale. They make an important contribution to the clean flavor of lager beer.

At the end of this chapter is the payoff — recipes for German and Belgian ales, as well as for many types of lager beer. The ales are more forgiving, and the only advanced technique that is absolutely required is the use of the pure yeast culture. But they too will benefit from the other steps.

USING PURE YEAST CULTURES

Pure yeast cultures have finally made it possible for home brewers to make beers with the flavor and aroma of the best imported and microbrewed beers. The difference yeast can make is almost impossible to believe until you try it for yourself. This is why I feel that learning to use these yeasts is the most important advance you can make in your brewing.

Equipment

There are only four additional items of equipment that you will need for culturing yeast. The first is a supply of 1-pint glass canning jars, rings, and lids. The first step in using a pure-culture yeast is to grow enough of it to pitch in a 5-gallon batch of wort. The package you buy does not contain enough yeast cells to do the job. The yeast must be grown in sterile wort; thus, to make wort sterile, you must can it just as you would can peaches or tomatoes. You already have a 5-gallon kettle, so the only other equipment you need is the jars and lids. They are sold in discount and grocery stores.

The second item is a butane torch or cigarette lighter. This is used to flame-sterilize the mouths of jars and carboys when you transfer yeast or starters from one vessel to another. The third item is a half-gallon glass jug with a stopper and airlock to fit. This is your starter jar. The last item is a supply of sterile cotton balls, used for plugging the airlock.

Materials

Pure yeast cultures are available in 50-milliliter plastic or foil packets which can be activated without opening. This feature eliminates the danger of contamination at the critical early stage. These cultures have several advantages. First, they are pure: that is, they are free from bacteria and "wild" (not deliberate-ly cultured) strains of yeast; all dried yeasts are contaminated with bacteria to some extent. Second, strains of both ale and lager yeast are available which are derived from those used in commercial breweries. This makes it possible to select a yeast (sometimes two or three) that is perfectly suited to the style of beer you want to brew. For example, a Bavarian lager yeast is the logical choice if you want to make a Munich beer; on the other hand, a Danish yeast would be better for a light, dry pilsner.

Pure yeast cultures must be stored in the refrigerator and used within 6 months after they are manufactured. They come with a date stamp, so you do not have to guess about this as you do with dry yeast. The place where uncertainty comes in is the shipping. Because pure yeast cells come in a liquid medium they are very vulnerable to heat, and a trip across the country during hot weather will wipe them out. If you live in a place with warm summers, you should not order yeast cultures, either by mail or through your local homebrew supplier, at any time when the temperature is likely to exceed 80°F. If you must violate this rule, insist that the yeast be shipped in an insulated, waterproof container packed in ice.

Method

Success with pure yeast cultures comes down to two factors: planning and sanitation. Planning is important because you must get your yeast activated several days before your brewing session. Sanitation is important because you want to keep your culture pure while you work with it.

The first step is to make up some sterile wort. For each ale yeast, you need 1 pint of starter. The following recipe makes a dozen pints, which will last you quite a while. Boil 1½ gallons of water in a large kettle for 15 minutes. Shut off the heat and stir in 1 pound of pale dry malt extract. Bring back to a boil, add ¼ ounce of hop pellets (Hallertau or other noble type), and boil 15 minutes. Top up if necessary to restore volume to 1½ gallons or a little more. Let the wort settle for 10 minutes, then fill a dozen pint jars, set on the lids, and screw the rings on loosely. Set six of the jars in the bottom of your brew kettle and add hot water until the level is about 1 inch below the top of the canning jars. Bring the water to a boil and simmer, covered, for 30 minutes. Remove the jars carefully and screw the rings down finger-tight. Repeat with the remaining six jars. Let the jars cool overnight.

Twelve pints may be more wort than you think you need. You can divide the recipe in half if you wish. Sterile wort keeps indefinitely, but if any of your jars shows signs of spontaneous fermentation (lid popping, bubbles, and so forth) you must of course discard it, and look with suspicion on the remaining jars in the batch. The chances of this happening, however, are remote.

With a supply of sterile wort on hand, you are ready to activate your liquid yeast culture. The manufacturer's instructions usually suggest giving 1 day's incubation for each month since the date stamped on the package. In my experience, this formula is unreliable. I suggest activating the packet 3 days before your intended brewing session, unless it is very old, in which case give it 4 days. But, in any case, be ready to adjust your plans. You cannot brew until your yeast is ready.

To activate the yeast, you must break the inner plastic bag, which contains a concentrated wort. Once this wort is released, the yeast will start absorbing nutrients and fermenting the sugars. The trick is to break the inner bag without rupturing the outer walls of the package. Some experts recommend setting the packet on a tabletop and applying pressure with the heel of your hand. This may be safer than smacking it, as the instructions say. But you must be sure the inner bag is actually broken.

Once you break the inner bag, it is very important to shake the packet vigorously for 5 minutes. This not only mixes the wort into the yeast, but also aerates it. Yeast needs air for growth and will not ferment satisfactorily unless the culture medium (wort) is thoroughly aerated at the beginning.

The packet should be kept at warm room temperature (around

Figure 2–1. A liquid yeast "smack pack" before the inner bag of wort is broken (left) and afterward (right), as the yeast starts to work and the bag begins to swell.

75°F.). Continue to shake it periodically (every hour or two) until it swells up. This will take 1 to 2 days with a fresh yeast. Then you are ready to make a starter culture. Sanitize your jug, airlock, bottle opener, a pair of scissors, a funnel, and the yeast package itself, in chlorine solution. Just before use, rinse everything in sterile water. If your tap water is not trustworthy, use cool boiled water for this. Open the jar of sterile wort, flame-sterilize the mouth of the jar, and funnel the wort into the jug. Shake the yeast packet well, cut it open, and pour the contents into the wort. Swirl or shake the jug for at least 2 minutes, to aerate as much as possible. Fit the airlock, but, rather than fill it with water, plug it with a sterile cotton ball. Swirl the starter vigorously for 2 minutes every hour or so for the next 8 hours. The following day it

should be fermenting vigorously, and be ready to pitch. Just before pitching, swirl the starter to resuspend all the yeast, and flame the mouth of the jug before adding it to the wort.

What if your yeast packet swells up sooner than anticipated? The best thing is to move your brewing session up, if possible. If not, you can refrigerate the packet as suggested in the instructions. Remember, though, to do this before the packet is at the bursting point. Fermentation will still continue, though more slowly, in the refrigerator.

The preceding paragraphs describe a single-step, 1-pint starter, suitable for ale yeast. For lager yeast, I recommend a two-stage starter procedure. This is exactly the same as the one-step, except that the activated packet of yeast is pitched into 1 cup (½ pint) of sterile wort. (Note: If you only have full pint jars, use half a jar and discard the remaining wort.) When this is fermenting vigorously, add 1 quart (2 pints) of sterile wort and continue to aerate periodically until this larger starter comes into vigorous fermentation before pitching. The extra step means an extra day, but you get a larger quantity of yeast, which is important because lagers are fermented at cooler temperatures than ales.

The same two-stage procedure is recommended for culturing yeast from bottles of naturally carbonated commercial beers (for example, Chimay Trappist ale). The only difference in the technique is that you first decant the beer, then funnel the cup of sterile wort into the bottle, flame the mouth, cover with plastic wrap, and shake well for 2 minutes. Then plug the bottle mouth with a ball of sterile cotton. Aerate this starter by swirling it several times a day. It may take as long as a week for fermentation to start. If the wort is not going by then, you have to assume the yeast in the bottle was dead. Try again with another bottle

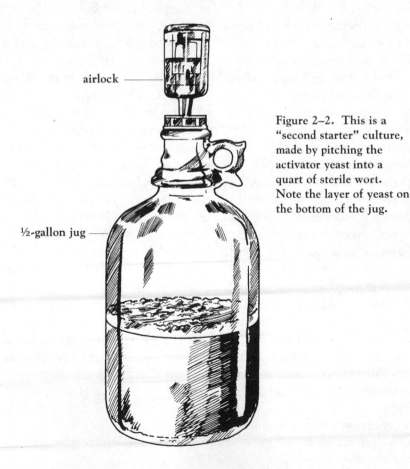

airlock

½-gallon jug

Figure 2–2. This is a "second starter" culture, made by pitching the activator yeast into a quart of sterile wort. Note the layer of yeast on the bottom of the jug.

from a different source. If the bottle kicks in, build up the culture in a quart of sterile wort and use this larger culture to pitch your batch of homebrew.

REPITCHING YEAST

Because pure yeast cultures are fairly expensive, most home brewers try to get several batches of beer out of each packet. This should not be tried with dry yeasts, because all of them are contaminated to some extent and the bacteria count will increase with each repitching. But with pure yeast cultures and good sanitation, repitching works fine.

The basic method of repitching is as follows. After racking your beer into the 5-gallon carboy, swirl the fermenter to loosen the yeast on the bottom. If you are using a glass fermenter, flame the mouth. Pour the dregs into a sanitized pint jar, cover the top with plastic wrap, and screw the lid on loosely. Store this jar on the bottom shelf of your refrigerator. Repitch within 3 days.

To repitch, first flame the mouth of the jar. Pour off the layer of beer on top and discard. Add about ½ cup (for ales) or ⅔ cup (for lagers) of the creamy slurry to the freshly cooled wort. Do not empty the jar. The bottom layer of yeast is darker and contains *trub* (see Glossary) and other materials that should be left behind.

An additional step that you can do before repitching is washing your yeast. This removes trub and other material that clings to the yeast cells. It will give even better results. Professional brewers use an acid wash, which kills contaminating bacteria. This is too dangerous for amateurs, but washing with plain water is useful, especially with lager yeasts.

Yeast to be washed must first be given 12 hours storage in the refrigerator. To wash yeast, first sanitize a quart jar. Fill with boiling water, screw on the lid loosely, and set in the refrigerator to cool overnight. The next day, flame the mouth of your yeast jar and pour off about half of the contents. Fill the jar with some of your cold water and stir thoroughly, using a sanitized spoon. Replace the lid, then put the jar and remaining water back in the refrigerator. Repeat this procedure after 8 to 12 hours, then again about 8 to 12 hours later. The yeast should be pitched about 8 hours after its final washing. To pitch, first pour off the semiclear liquid on top, then flame the mouth of the jar and add the grayish tan yeast slurry to the freshly cooled wort. It is better to leave the bottom layer in the jar, as it may still contain some trub; however, lager yeasts tend to be sticky, and you may have to stir the slurry in order to get enough yeast out of the jar.

Repitching is limited. Do not go through more than five generations (batches) with one yeast culture. If you do, your yeast may get tired and perform badly, especially with lager yeast.

I do not recommend repitching

yeasts grown from a bottle of naturally carbonated beer.

FULL WORT BOIL AND WORT COOLING

A full wort boil simply means making up your wort to the total volume of your batch, plus some extra to allow for boiloff. The advantage is that all of the wort is sterilized shortly before pitching. An additional benefit with pale beers is that the thinner the wort, the less it will darken during the boil. The full boil demands forced cooling, which tends to give a better break (the coagula-

tion of proteins and other insoluble material).

Equipment

1. Wort chiller. This is a do-it-yourself item, made from 50 feet of ⅜-inch outside diameter (o.d.) flexible copper tubing, available from building supply stores. You also need a couple of 4-foot lengths (or longer, depending on your kitchen layout) of 5/16-inch inside diameter (i.d.) flexible clear plastic tubing (same as racking hose), plus step-up adapters and clamps and a larger piece of tubing that can be fitted

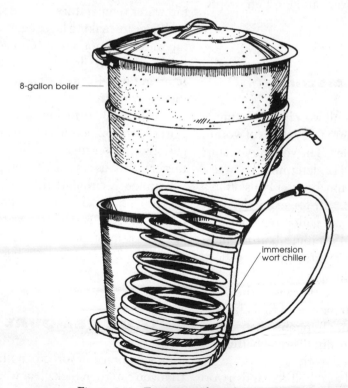

8-gallon boiler

immersion wort chiller

Figure 2–3. Equipment for a full wort boil.

with a threaded nipple and attached to the kitchen faucet. The copper tubing is formed into a coil that will fit inside your boiler. Figure 2–4 shows a typical assembly. Constructing one of these homemade chillers takes about an hour. To use it, cold water is circulated through the tubing to chill the wort right after boiling.

2. Large boiler. This is a natural complement to a wort chiller. With a chiller, you can easily bring 5 gallons of wort down to pitching temperature in less than an hour. The cheapest large boiler is a 33-quart enamelware canner, available at homebrew supply stores and some hardware and kitchen supply stores.

Method

Going to a full wort boil is as simple as making up 5 to 6 gallons of wort in a larger boiler. The volume you start with should be determined by a test to see how much water boils off in a given time. If, for example, your boiloff rate is 1 gallon per hour, and you use a 45-minute boil for most beers, then if you start with 6 gallons you will end up with 5.25, which is just right. Otherwise, the only change you may need to make is to decrease your hop rates slightly, because hop resins dissolve better in a more diluted wort.

The full wort boil demands a wort chiller. The immersion type de-scribed here is easy to use. About 10 minutes before the end of the boil, remove the lid, insert the cooler, and recover the kettle. Be careful not to touch the plastic hoses to the metal sides of the boiler or get them near the fire — they may melt or even burst into flames. This 10-minute stand in boiling wort destroys any bacteria that may be clinging to the copper and eliminates the need for sanitizing.

At the end of the boil, move the boiler to a counter next to your sink. Hook up the inlet hose to the faucet and put the outlet hose in the sink. Start circulating cold water through the tubing. In 30 minutes the wort should be within 10 degrees of the tap water temperature.

If you are making lager beer, your tap water may not be cool enough to bring the wort down to pitching temperature (46° to 54°F., depending upon the recipe). In this case, you will have to make up an ice-water bath (32 pounds of ice and 4 gallons of water in a 15-gallon container) and use a small pump to continuously circulate this cold water through the chiller. The proper technique is to use your tap water to get rid of most of the heat; then, after 20 or 25 minutes, switch to the ice water.

TRUB REMOVAL

One advantage of forced cooling is that you can then rack clear wort off the trub (break material) before fermentation begins. This is desirable because it will give you a clearer and cleaner-tasting beer.

Equipment

1. Glass primary fermenter. For trub removal you will need two primary fermenters, so now is the logical time to invest in a 7-gallon glass carboy. Glass is preferred by advanced home brewers because it is easier to sanitize than plastic and cheaper in the long run. Plastic fermenters and other plastic equipment, such as racking tubes and hoses, must be replaced every 3 or 4 years because they eventually become impossible to clean thoroughly. Seven-gallon carboys can be found at many homebrew supply stores. They take the same stoppers and airlocks as the 5-gallon carboys.

2. Strainer. This is not necessary if you are using pelletized hops, but it enables you to use whole hops if you wish. An alternative to a con-

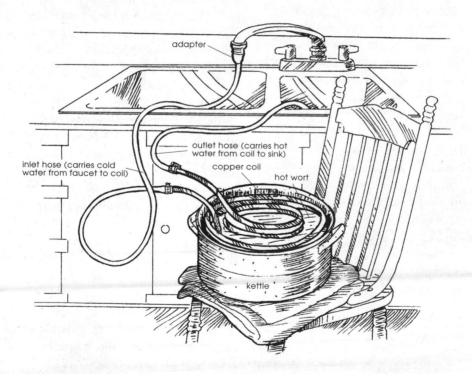

Figure 2–4. Cooling the hot wort with an immersion chiller. The inlet hose is connected to the faucet and carries cold water to the cooler. As it flows through the coil, the water picks up heat from the wort and then flows back to the sink through the outlet hose.

ventional strainer is to insert the end of a racking tube into a nylon scouring pad. The wort can then be racked out of the boiler without clogging the tube.

Method

After cooling the wort in the boiler to pitching temperature, remove the wort chiller and cover the kettle while you sanitize your fermenting bucket and strainer. Then strain the wort into it. Immediately pitch your yeast starter or slurry and fit the lid. Aerate by vigorous stirring or shaking for 5 minutes. Repeat this every hour for 5 hours after pitching. Put the fermenter, which should now be called your *starter tank*, in your basement or (for lagers) your fermenting refrigerator.

Twelve hours after pitching, sanitize your 7-gallon carboy, racking tube, and hose. Once they are sanitized, handle them carefully. Remove the lid of your starter tank and very gently insert the racking tube. Siphon the wort into your carboy, leaving at least a pint of trub-laden wort at the bottom of the tank. Sanitize an airlock and stopper and fit as usual.

TOP-FERMENTATION TECHNIQUE

Some ale yeasts available in pure cultures are true "top fermenters."

This means that when the yeast *flocculates* (forms clumps) in the wort, it rises to the top rather than settling to the bottom. Wyeast Labs' #1007 is one example.

The problem with such yeasts is that the dense foamy head of flocculated yeast cells must be removed before it collapses. Otherwise those billions of yeast cells will be resuspended in the beer, which will be grossly clouded and take months to clear.

If you are using a plastic fermenter with a lid, removing the yeast head is as simple as skimming it off with a spoon. However, if you have switched to glass (as I recommend), you will need to rack the beer from one vessel to another when the head has reached its peak and is just beginning to recede.

Top-fermenting yeasts are especially likely to overflow the headspace in a 7-gallon carboy, so you may need to fit a blowoff tube as described in Chapter 1 (see page 20). The best time to rack is as soon as the yeast stops blowing out of the tube.

You may find that, even with skimming or racking, some top-fermenting yeasts take a terribly long time to clear. In this case consider adding *isinglass finings*. Isinglass is a natural protein product that attaches to the yeast cells and helps them settle out more quickly. It is available from most homebrew shops and should be made up and used as recommended by your supplier. The best time to add it is at bottling.

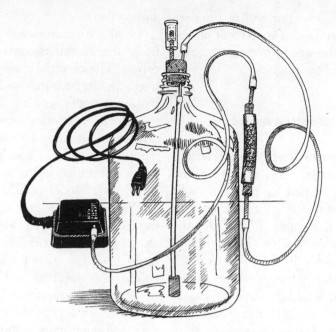

Figure 2–5. A wort aeration assembly. The wort aerator consists of a cork fitted with an airlock and a length of ¼-inch copper tubing. The copper tube is attached to a length of polyethlene tubing, which in turn connects to an aquarium aeration stone. In use, the aerator is inserted into the starting tank.

WORT AERATION

If you have made a couple of batches of homebrew, you are probably already tired of all the shaking or stirring you have to do after pitching the yeast. Aeration is terribly important to a successful fermentation, but it is tiring and, in the case of stirring, dangerous because opening the starter tank exposes the wort to possible contamination from airborne bacteria and wild yeasts.

Wort can be thoroughly aerated using a simple device which you can either buy or make for yourself (see Figure 2–5). To use this wort aerator, simply insert it into the airlock opening in your starter tank and let the pump run until the headspace is full of foam. Repeat this every hour for 5 hours after pitching. Then remove the device and let the wort settle for about 7 hours before racking the wort off into your fermenter.

LAGER FERMENTATION AND AGING

In brewing lager beers, a different species of yeast (*Saccharomyces carlbergensis*), capable of fermenting the wort at cool temperatures, is used. This yeast will work at warmer temperatures, too, but will not impart the clean flavor expected of lagers. Hence the need for special equipment and techniques.

Equipment

Refrigerator. Refrigeration is necessary for the aging of lager beers, which is carried out at 32 to 34°F. Furthermore, if your basement is warmer than around 50°F. in winter, or if you want to brew all year round, you will also need to use a refrigerator for fermentation. In this case, you should check your refrigerator's thermostat to make sure it will maintain temperatures as high as 46° to 54°F. If not, you can buy and install an external thermostat that will do the job.

Used refrigerators are available from private sellers at reasonable prices. The external thermostat (if needed) can be purchased at most building supply stores. They are made for programming room air conditioners, but have a remote temperature sensor that can be placed inside the fridge. One example is the Hunter Model 42205.

People who do a lot of lager brewing will probably need two refrigerators: one for fermentation set at 46° to 54°F. and another for aging and cold storage (lagering) at 32°F. This second refrigerator has to have a lot of space. It is possible to expand your refrigerator by removing the door and building out the walls another 3 or 4 feet, using plywood

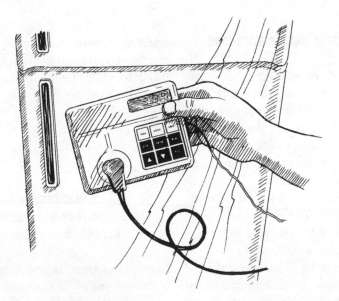

Figure 2–6. An external thermometer is used to control the temperature of a fermenting refrigerator.

Figure 2–7. You can enlarge a refrigerator for use in brewing by building a plywood addition to the lower compartment and insulating the box with 2-inch rigid Styrofoam paneling.

lined with insulating panels. Figure 2–7 shows an example.

Because a brewing refrigerator is not opened frequently, doubling or tripling the space inside it will not significantly increase the load on the compressor. There is no need to worry about this.

Method

Lager fermentation requires low temperatures and a long time. Especially if you began with a 1-quart starter culture, it can take 2 weeks for the beer to ferment. The actual time must be determined by observation.

When the beer is fermented out (the bubbling of the airlock is down to once every 60 seconds), rack the beer into the secondary fermenter (5-gallon carboy) and let it sit for about a week before bottling. After bottling, store the beer for a week at fermentation temperature before lowering the temperature — to 32° to 34°F., ideally — for *lagering* (cold storage).

One thing you should be aware of is that lager yeast does not ferment as spectacularly as ale yeast. Usually all you will see is a head of white foam 1 to 2 inches thick, and this head may disappear well before fermentation is over.

There are two special types of yeast that require modifications of the basic fermentation method. American lager yeasts should be fermented at a slightly warmer temperature — about 55°F. Lagering also may take place at this temperature. Times are also shorter: 5 to 7 days for fermentation, 3 weeks for aging.

With Weihenstephan #308 yeast (Wyeast Labs #2308), you should ferment about a week at 46°F., then allow the temperature to rise to 60° or 65°F. for the second week. Then rack and store at 32°F., as usual. This procedure may also be employed with other lager yeasts if you encounter problems with a butterscotch flavor (indicating the presence of diacetyl) or a green-apple flavor (acetaldehyde); the high-temperature stage helps eliminate these unwanted by-products from the finished beer.

If your basement is cold enough (54°F. or lower), it is possible to ferment lagers in the winter without using a refrigerator. Cold storage is likewise possible if a cool enough space (40°F.) is available.

INTRODUCTION TO ADVANCED EXTRACT RECIPES

There are two things you should be aware of when you prepare these recipes. The first is that some of them are based on special new malt extracts that are made from a blend of malts. These extracts have been developed especially for microbreweries and will give superior results. Do not substitute other brands. However, dry and syrup forms of the same extract may be substituted for one another on this basis: 1 pound of

dry malt extract is equivalent to 1.33 pounds of syrup; 1 pound of malt extract syrup is equivalent to ¾ pound of dry.

The second thing to consider is that these recipes give the option of using whole or pelletized hops. Although everybody agrees that pellets are more convenient to use, some commercial and home brewers continue to prefer the unprocessed type. Different hop rates are given because pellets yield more of their bitterness in the wort. If you would like to use whole hops with some of the ale recipes in Chapter 1, just multiply the AAUs given by 1.2. This will compensate for the lower bitterness yield (called *utilization* in brewers' jargon).

NOTES ON THE BEERS

The following recipes represent most of the established commercial beer styles that are currently produced. A few are intentionally omitted, most notably Gueze/Lambic, the famous "wild beer" of Belgium. Those wishing to attempt this style need more guidance than a general home brewing book can provide; I recommend reading *Lambic* by Jean-Xavier Guinard (listed in the Bibliography). Now, to describe the rest:

Alt means 'old' in German, and **altbier** is the old style (that is, ale, as opposed to the newfangled lager) of dark German beer. It is hoppy, malty, and full-flavored. Pinkus Mueller is one brand that is sometimes available here, but it is lighter and less bitter than most examples. **Kolsch,** brewed in the region around Cologne (Köln), is basically the pale variety of alt. It is lightly hopped, malty, and fruity, with some occasional acidic undertones. It is almost unknown in this country.

German wheat beers come in two distinct varieties: **weiss,** from northern Germany, and **weizen,** from the south. They differ in many ways. Weiss is a low-gravity brew (1.032), made with 25 percent wheat malt, and it has a very tart flavor produced by deliberately inoculating (infecting?) the wort with lactic-acid–producing bacteria. Kindl is one brand that is sometimes available here. Weizen is made by all the major Bavarian breweries, including Spaten and Paulaner. Just to confuse things, they often label it "weiss," but it is a different thing entirely. It is a normal strength beer (1.045), made with 50 to 67 percent wheat malt, and always has a definite clovelike aroma and flavor produced by special strains of yeast that are used only for this type of beer.

Wit is a very pale Belgian wheat beer. Its distinction arises largely from the use of coriander instead of hops for aroma. The best-known brand, fairly widely available, is Hoegaarden. Another Belgian specialty is the strong ale produced by a number of **Trappist** monasteries. These beers derive much of their flavor from the mixed cultures (several different strains) of yeast used in their fermentation. The best known is Chimay, which is made in three different strengths. Then there are the famous Belgian fruit ales, **peche** (made with peaches), **kriek** (cherries), and **framboise** (raspberries). All are based on the difficult lambic style, but they can be imitated by using simpler methods. Lindeman's and Liefman's are both available in the United States.

Cream ale is an American original, pale and dry like conventional American beer, but originally made by blending batches fermented with ale and lager yeast. For simplicity, I suggest brewing it with a clean, neutral-flavored ale yeast.

California common beer flourished in the late nineteenth century; today only a single commercial example survives, made by a famous San Francisco brewery. Recipes were apparently quite variable, but the modern version is similar to pale ale — amber in color, malty, and quite bitter. It is made using lager yeast, but is fermented at ale temperatures. This unique fermentation method was an American invention and gives the style its distinct place among the beers of the world.

Pilsner was not the original lager beer, but it is by a long chalk the most successful. First brewed in Bohemia in 1842, this pale, dry, hoppy style quickly spread across the beer-drinking world. In many countries, including the United States, the hop character has been toned down considerably. If you have never tried anything but American Pilsner, by all means try a few of the lighter European brands (such as Carlsberg from Denmark), and some of the all-malt German and Czech brews as well. Pilsner Urquell, the original Pilsner, is a masterpiece (if you can find a fresh example), but a number of German "pils" are also worth seeking out, including Warsteiner and DAB.

Munich is where lager brewing began, and the pale **(helles)** and dark **(dunkel)** styles are similar in being lightly hopped, with a full malt body and flavor. Excellent examples of both are available in this country, brewed by Paulaner, Hacker-Pschorr, and Spaten, among others. On the other hand, genuine **Dortmunder Export** is hard to find. Most Dortmund beer on dealers' shelves is actually of the Pilsner style. The Kronen brand is sometimes available. It is basically a higher-gravity, very full-flavored cousin of Munich helles.

Oktoberfest beer is an amber-colored, high-gravity Munich beer. It is also called **Märzen** or, in a lower-gravity manifestation, **Vienna.** It is the special beer of the famous annual celebration. You can get it over here, in season, without too much trouble.

Like Munich, **bock** beer comes in two varieties, the dark one associated with winter and early spring, the pale with late spring (it is sometimes called **Maibock).** Both are very strong, heavy, malty, and sweet. A number of brands are available. All the authentic ones come from Bavaria; in other countries, almost any dark beer may be called a bock. **Doppelbock** is an even stronger variation of dark bock. German doppelbocks are easy to identify because all their names end in *-ator* (Celebrator, Kulminator, etc.).

SUMMARY OF THE ADVANCED EXTRACT BREWING METHOD

The nine steps below incorporate all the advanced techniques described in this chapter. Use these in conjunction with the specifics given in each recipe.

1. Prepare yeast starter, if necessary.

2. Crush specialty grains (if used), put in a mesh bag, and steep in brewing water at about 160°F. for 30 minutes. Remove.

3. Dissolve malt extracts in brewing water and bring wort to a boil. Boil 45 minutes total. Add hops as specified in recipe.

4. Shut off heat. Cool wort to temperature specified in recipe. Strain off whole hops (if used).

5. Pitch yeast starter or yeast slurry (½ cup slurry for ale yeast, ⅔ cup slurry for lager yeast.) Aerate the wort thoroughly.

6. After 8 hours, rack beer into another fermenter, leaving behind as much trub as possible. Affix airlock.

7. For all lagers, and for ales pitched with bottom-fermenting yeast, allow the beer to ferment out.

7a. Optional, for beers pitched with top fermenting yeast: Allow to ferment for 2 to 3 days, until the *kraeusen* (the large head of foam) reaches a maximum and is just beginning to fall. Rack into another fermenter and allow the beer to ferment out.

8. When fermentation is over, rack into a 5-gallon carboy and allow the beer to settle for at least 5 days. Make up your priming sugar syrup. Rack the beer into a bottling tank (a sanitized plastic bucket or glass fermenter) and add the syrup. Also, for ales, add isinglass finings if desired. Bottle.

9. Store at the appropriate temperature for the time specified in the recipe.

RECIPES

All recipes yield approximately 5 gallons (U.S.) of beer.

ALTBIER (DARK GERMAN ALE)

Specialty grains: 8 oz. 40°L. crystal malt; plus 1 oz. black malt

Malt extract: 2 lbs. Briess Weizen dry, unhopped; plus 3.5 lbs. Briess amber dry, unhopped. (Note: In syrup form, Briess extracts are also sold as "Northwestern.")

Bittering hops: 8 AAUs pellets or 10 AAUs whole Hallertau, Tettnanger, Spalt, or Perle

Finishing hops: none

Yeast: Wyeast Labs #1007 or #1338, or M.eV. Research #3

Priming sugar: ¾ cup corn sugar

Gravities: original gravity 1.047; terminal gravity about 1.014

Brewer's Specifics

1. Add two-thirds of hops at beginning of boil; add remaining third 15 minutes before the end.
2. Pitching and fermentation temperature: 60–65°F.
3. Store 1 week at room temperature, then 4 weeks at 40–45°F.

KOLSCH (LIGHT GERMAN ALE)

Specialty grains: none

Malt extract: 4 lbs. Alexander's pale syrup, unhopped; plus 2 lbs. Laaglander pale dry, unhopped

Bittering hops: 5 AAUs pellets or 6 AAUs whole Hallertau, Tettnanger, Spalt, or Perle

Finishing hops: none

Yeast: Wyeast Labs #1007 or #1338, or M.eV. Research #3

Priming sugar: ¾ cup corn sugar

Gravities: original gravity 1.046; terminal gravity about 1.010

Brewer's Specifics:

1. Add two-thirds of hops at beginning of boil; add remaining third 15 minutes before the end.
2. Pitching and fermentation temperature: 60–65°F.
3. Store 1 week at room temperature, then 4 weeks at 40–45°F.

WEISSBIER (LIGHT-BODIED GERMAN WHEAT BEER)

Specialty grains: none
Malt extract: 2 lbs. Briess Weizen dry, unhopped; plus 2 lbs. Briess pale dry, unhopped
Bittering hops: 3.5 AAUs pellets or 4 AAUs whole Hallertau, Tettnanger, Spalt, or Perle
Finishing hops: none
Yeast: Wyeast Labs #1007 or #1338, or M.eV. Research #3
Priming sugar: ¾ cup corn sugar
Gravities: original gravity 1.034; terminal gravity about 1.005

Brewer's Specifics

1. Add two-thirds of hops at beginning of boil; add remaining third 15 minutes before the end.
2. Pitching and fermentation temperature: 60–65°F.
3. For the tartness of a true Berliner Weissbier, add food-grade lactic acid to taste at bottling.
4. Store 1 week at room temperature, then 4 weeks at 40–45°F.

WEIZENBIER

Specialty grains: none
Malt extract: 6.6 lbs. Briess Weizen syrup, unhopped. (Note: In syrup form, Briess extracts are also sold as "Northwestern.")
Bittering hops: 5 AAUs pellets or 6 AAUs whole Hallertau, Tettnanger, Spalt, or Perle
Finishing hops: none
Yeast: Wyeast Labs #3056 or M.eV. Research #33
Priming sugar: 1 cup corn sugar
Gravities: original gravity 1.046; terminal gravity about 1.010

Brewer's Specifics

1. Add two-thirds of hops at beginning of boil; add remaining third 15 minutes before the end.
2. Pitching and fermentation temperature: 60–65°F.
3. Store 1 week at room temperature, then 4 weeks at 40–45°F.

WIT (BELGIAN WHEAT BEER)

Specialty grains: none
Malt extract: 3.3 lbs. Briess Weizen syrup, unhopped; plus 2 lbs. Laaglander pale dry, unhopped. (Note: In syrup form, Briess extracts are also sold as "Northwestern.")
Bittering hops: 4 AAUs pellets or 5 AAUs whole Hallertau, Tettnanger, Spalt, or Perle
Finishing hops: none
Yeast: Wyeast Labs #1007 or #1338, or M.eV. Research #69
Special ingredient: 1 oz. coriander seed
Priming sugar: 1 cup corn sugar
Gravities: original gravity 1.041; terminal gravity about 1.008

Brewer's Specifics

1. Add two-thirds of hops at beginning of boil; add remaining third 15 minutes before the end.
2. Pitching and fermentation temperature: 60–65°F.
3. Crush the coriander and add to the 5-gallon carboy just before racking. Leave the beer in the carboy for 10 days before bottling.
4. Store 1 week at room temperature, then 4 weeks at 40–45°F.

TRAPPIST ALE

Specialty grains: 1 lb. 40°L. crystal malt; plus ½ oz. black malt
Malt extract: 6.6 lbs. British pale syrup, unhopped; plus 3 lbs. Briess amber dry, unhopped
Sugar: 1 lb. dark brown sugar (add to wort)
Bittering hops: 11 AAUs pellets or 13 AAUs whole Fuggles, Northern Brewer, Goldings, or Hallertau, or a blend
Finishing hops: none
Yeast: Cultured from a bottle of Chimay ale
Priming sugar: ½ cup corn sugar
Gravities: original gravity 1.078; terminal gravity about 1.020

Brewer's Specifics

1. Add two-thirds of hops at beginning of boil; add remaining third 15 minutes before the end.
2. Pitching and fermentation temperature: 70–75°F.
3. Store 1 week at room temperature, then 8 weeks at 45–50°F.

FRUIT ALE

Specialty grains: none
Malt extract: 6.6 lbs. Briess Weizen syrup, unhopped
Bittering hops: 2 AAUs pellets or whole Fuggles or Willamette
Finishing hops: none
Yeast: Wyeast Labs #1007 or #1338, or M.eV. Research #3
Special ingredient: 8–12 lbs. fruit, washed and crushed: peaches, cherries, or raspberries (used in second fermentation)
Acid blend (optional): A blend of citric, malic, and tartaric acids, available at winemaking supply stores.
Priming sugar: 1 cup corn sugar
Gravities: original gravity 1.046; terminal gravity about 1.010

Brewer's Specifics

1. Add two-thirds of hops at beginning of boil; add remaining third 15 minutes before the end.
2. Pitching and fermentation temperature: 60–65°F.
3. Crush the fruit and add to a second 7-gallon carboy just before racking. Allow the beer to ferment for at least a month before racking again.
4. If necessary, the tartness of the beer may be increased by adding winemaker's acid blend just before bottling.
5. Store 1 week at room temperature, then 4 weeks at 40–45°F.

CREAM ALE

Specialty grains: none

Malt extract: 4 lbs. Alexander's pale syrup, unhopped; plus 1 lb. Laaglander pale dry, unhopped

Grain extract: 1 lb. dry rice extract

Bittering hops: 4 AAUs pellets or 5 AAUs whole Hallertau, Tettnanger, Spalt, or Cascade

Finishing hops: ¼ oz. Hallertau, Tettnanger, or Cascade

Yeast: Wyeast Labs #1056 or M.eV. Research #69

Priming sugar: ¾ cup corn sugar

Gravities: original gravity 1.045; terminal gravity about 1.009

Brewer's Specifics

1. Add bittering hops 30 minutes before the end of the boil. Add finishing hops 5 minutes before the end.

2. Pitching and fermentation temperature: 60–65°F.

3. Store 1 week at room temperature, then 4 weeks at 40–45°F.

CALIFORNIA COMMON BEER

Specialty grains: 12 oz. 40°L. crystal malt

Malt extract: 3.3 lbs. Briess pale syrup, unhopped; plus 3.3 lbs. Briess amber syrup, unhopped. (Note: In syrup form, Briess extracts are also sold as "Northwestern.")

Bittering hops: 10 AAUs pellets or 12 AAUs whole Northern Brewer or Cascade

Finishing hops: 1 oz. Cascade or Northern Brewer

Yeast: Wyeast Labs #2007 or M.eV. Research #4

Priming sugar: ¾ cup corn sugar

Gravities: original gravity 1.046; terminal gravity about 1.010

Brewer's Specifics

1. Add bittering hops at the beginning of the boil. Add finishing hops 5 minutes before the end.
2. Pitching and fermentation temperature: 60–65°F.
3. Store 1 week at room temperature, then 4 weeks at 32–40°F.

AMERICAN PILSNER

Specialty grains: none
Malt extract: 4 lbs. Alexander's pale syrup, unhopped; plus 1 lb. Laaglander pale dry, unhopped
Grain extract: 1 lb. dry rice extract
Bittering hops: 4 AAUs pellets or 5 AAUs whole Cascade or other noble hops
Finishing hops: ½ oz. Cascade or other noble hops
Yeast: Wyeast Labs #2007 or M.eV. Research #4
Priming sugar: ¾ cup corn sugar
Gravities: original gravity 1.045; terminal gravity about 1.010

Brewer's Specifics

1. Add bittering hops 30 minutes before the end of the boil. Add finishing hops 5 minutes before the end.
2. Pitching and fermentation temperature: 50–55°F.
3. Store 10 days at fermentation temperature, then 4 weeks at 32–40°F.

LIGHT CONTINENTAL PILSNER

Follow the preceding recipe for American Pilsner, but increase the hop rate to 7 AAUs (pellets) or 8 AAUs (whole hops) and use German noble hops or Saaz. For finishing hops use 1 oz. Saaz. Recommended yeast is Wyeast Labs #2042; recommended fermentation temperature is 50°F.

ALL-MALT CONTINENTAL PILSNER

Specialty grains: 4 oz. 20°L. crystal malt (optional)
Malt extract: 4 lbs. Alexander's pale syrup, unhopped; plus 2.5 lbs.
  Laaglander pale dry, unhopped
Bittering hops: 10 AAUs pellets or 12 AAUs whole Hallertau or Tettnanger
Finishing hops: 1 to 1.5 oz. Saaz
Yeast: M.eV. Research #37 or #55, or Wyeast Labs #2042 or #2308 (see note
  at end of recipe)
Priming sugar: ¾ cup corn sugar
Gravities: original gravity 1.049; terminal gravity about 1.012

Brewer's Specifics

1. Add bittering hops 30 minutes before the end of the boil. Add finishing hops 5 minutes before the end.
2. Pitching and fermentation temperature: 45–50°F.
3. Store 14 days at fermentation temperature, then 5 weeks at 32–40°F.

A note on yeast: The type of yeast chosen will influence the flavor even more than with other beer styles. For a clean, malty flavor, use M.eV. #37. For a more complex character with a hint of butterscotch (diacetyl), similar to Pilsner Urquell, use Wyeast #2308 and do *not* use the high-temperature rest described earlier in this chapter (see page 46). For a lighter flavor, use Wyeast #2042 or M.eV. #55.

MUNICH HELLES (PALE)

Specialty grains: none

Malt extract: 3 lbs. Laaglander pale dry, unhopped; plus 2 lbs. Briess pale dry, unhopped

Bittering hops: 5 AAUs pellets or 6 AAUs whole Hallertau or Tettnanger

Finishing hops: ¼ oz. Hallertau or Tettnanger

Yeast: M.eV. Research #37, or Wyeast Labs #2206 or #2308 (use a high-temperature rest with #2308; see discussion on page 46)

Priming sugar: ¾ cup corn sugar

Gravities: original gravity 1.045; terminal gravity about 1.012

Brewer's Specifics

1. Add bittering hops 30 minutes before the end of the boil. Add finishing hops 5 minutes before the end.
2. Pitching and fermentation temperature: 45–50°F.
3. Store 14 days at fermentation temperature, then 5 weeks at 32–40°F.

MUNICH DUNKEL (DARK)

Specialty grains: 8 oz. 60°L. crystal malt; plus 1 oz. black malt

Malt extract: 6.6 lbs. Briess amber syrup, unhopped (also sold as "Northwestern" brand)

Bittering hops: 5 AAUs pellets or 6 AAUs whole Hallertau or Tettnanger

Finishing hops: none

Yeast: M.eV. Research #37, or Wyeast Labs #2206 or #2308

Priming sugar: ¾ cup corn sugar

Gravities: original gravity 1.046; terminal gravity about 1.012

Brewer's Specifics

1. Add two-thirds of hops at beginning of boil; add remaining third 15 minutes before the end.
2. Pitching and fermentation temperature: 45–50°F.
3. Store 14 days at fermentation temperature, then 5 weeks at 32–40°F.

DORTMUNDER EXPORT

Specialty grains: 4 oz. 20°L. crystal malt
Malt extract: 6.6 lbs. Briess pale syrup, unhopped (also sold as
   "Northwestern" brand); plus 1 lb. Laaglander pale dry, unhopped
Bittering hops: 6 AAUs pellets or 7 AAUs whole Hallertau or Tettnanger
Finishing hops: none
Yeast: M.eV. Research #37, or Wyeast Labs #2206 or #2308
Priming sugar: ¾ cup corn sugar
Gravities: original gravity 1.055; terminal gravity about 1.014

Brewer's Specifics

1. Add two-thirds of hops at beginning of boil; add remaining third 15
    minutes before the end.
2. Pitching and fermentation temperature: 45–50°F.
3. Store 14 days at fermentation temperature, then 6 weeks at 32–40°F.

OKTOBERFEST (MÄRZENBIER)

Specialty grains: 4 oz. 40°L. crystal malt
Malt extract: 6.6 lbs. Briess amber syrup, unhopped (also sold as
   "Northwestern" brand); plus 1 lb. Laaglander pale dry, unhopped
Bittering hops: 6 AAUs pellets or 7 AAUs whole Hallertau or Tettnanger
Finishing hops: none
Yeast: M.eV. Research #37, or Wyeast Labs #2206 or #2308
Priming sugar: ¾ cup corn sugar
Gravities: original gravity 1.055; terminal gravity about 1.014

Brewer's Specifics

1. Add two-thirds of hops at beginning of boil; add remaining third 15
    minutes before the end.
2. Pitching and fermentation temperature: 45–50°F.
3. Store 14 days at fermentation temperature, then 6 weeks at 32–40°F.

HELLES (PALE) BOCK

Specialty grains: 6 oz. 20°L. crystal malt
Malt extract: 6.6 lbs. Briess pale syrup, unhopped (also sold as
  "Northwestern" brand); plus 2 lbs. Laaglander pale dry, unhopped
Bittering hops: 7 AAUs pellets or 8 AAUs whole Hallertau or Tettnanger
Finishing hops: none
Yeast: M.eV. Research #37, or Wyeast Labs #2206 or #2308
Priming sugar: ¾ cup corn sugar
Gravities: original gravity 1.064; terminal gravity about 1.016

Brewer's Specifics

1. Add two-thirds of hops at beginning of boil; add remaining third 15
   minutes before the end.
2. Pitching and fermentation temperature: 45–50°F.
3. Store 14 days at fermentation temperature, then 8 weeks at 32–40°F.

DUNKEL (DARK) BOCK

Specialty grains: 2 lbs. 60°L. crystal malt
Malt extract: 3.3 lbs. Briess dark syrup, unhopped (also sold as
  "Northwestern" brand); plus 3.3 lbs. Briess amber syrup, unhopped; plus 2 lbs.
  Laaglander pale dry, unhopped
Bittering hops: 7 AAUs pellets or 8 AAUs whole Hallertau or Tettnanger
Finishing hops: none
Yeast: M.eV. Research #37, or Wyeast Labs #2206 or #2308
Priming sugar: ¾ cup corn sugar
Gravities: original gravity 1.066; terminal gravity about 1.017

Brewer's Specifics

1. Add two-thirds of hops at beginning of boil; add remaining third 15
   minutes before the end.
2. Pitching and fermentation temperature: 45–50°F.
3. Store 14 days at fermentation temperature, then 8 weeks at 32–40°F.

DOPPELBOCK

Follow the preceding recipe for Dunkel Bock, but increase the amount of Laaglander pale dry extract to 3 lbs. This will increase the original gravity to 1.075 and the terminal gravity to about 1.020.

FIRST STEPS IN GRAIN BREWING

If you have learned to handle pure yeast cultures, and adopted the other advanced techniques set out in Chapter 2, you are already making fine beer. To become a master brewer, the only step left is to brew your beer as the professionals do: from grain malt.

Grain brewing has a reputation for being difficult, but the fact is that the process is simple and has a lot of latitude built into it. Mainly it requires more time and equipment than extract brewing. In return, grain brewing offers economy — grain malt is less than half the price of malt extract — plus the opportunity to experiment and fine-tune the flavor profile of your beer exactly as you wish. Finally, a fresh malt aroma is an important part of the appeal of many beer styles, and it is only possible to get this characteristic from grain malt.

One way to get most of the benefits of grain brewing, with a minimum of investment and risk, is to follow what I call the "partial-mash technique," which uses grains to sup-plement an extract-based wort. This method allows you to "get your feet wet" before taking the plunge into all-grain brewing.

EQUIPMENT

The most important extra piece of equipment you need for a partial mash is a large *strainer* of some kind. This is used to separate the husks from the sweet wort after mashing. You can make a big strainer by drilling hundreds of 3/16-inch holes in the bottom of a 4-gallon plastic bucket. Such buckets are used for egg yolks and other food products and can be obtained from dairies and bakeries. Alternatively, a really big stainless steel or copper colander will also work.

Partial mashing requires a full wort boil, so if you have not already got one, you will need a larger kettle (minimum 8-gallon capacity) in addition to the smaller kettle you started out with.

You will also need a good *thermometer* to measure the temperature of the mash. You can get along with an inexpensive glass-bulb model, but a dial type is a modest investment and will make it easier to get repeatable results.

MATERIALS

In addition to the specialty malts you are already familiar with, you will be using the regular *malts* that

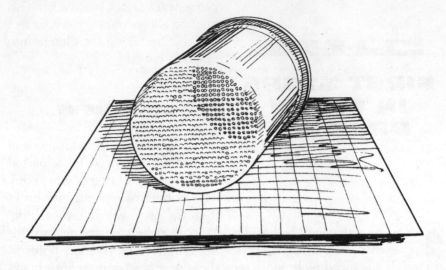

Figure 3–1. An excellent strainer can be made by drilling hundreds of ³⁄₁₆-inch holes in the bottom of a 4-gallon, food-grade plastic bucket.

form the backbone of all beers. These malts contain starches which, during the mash, will be converted to malt sugars. Several varieties of malt are available, including six-row pale, two-row pale, pale ale, mild ale, Vienna, Munich, and wheat. They all have different flavors and aromas and should not be substituted for one another.

Adjuncts are specially processed starchy grains that can be used in the mash along with malt. American breweries use corn or rice, for example, to lighten the body and color of their beer. Other grains create other characteristics in the final product: for example, flaked raw barley adds smoothness to dry stout.

Water is not a new ingredient, of course, but grain brewers need to pay closer attention to their water supply than extract brewers. This is because the chemistry of the brewing water influences the mash process in a number of ways. The particulars are spelled out in some detail in my *Complete Handbook of Home Brewing* (Garden Way Publishing, 1988). For a beginning masher, though, the "whys" are not so important as the "whats."

You will first have to make a call to your local water company and ask for someone in the lab who can answer some basic questions. All municipal water supplies are regularly tested to comply with state and federal standards. Only two items are really important to you as a home brewer:

1. Calcium ions. This reading should be between 50 and 100 parts per million (ppm). If it is lower, you may have to add calcium when you brew all-grain beers. However, for partial mashes, the amount is not really critical. The main reason for getting this information now is to save yourself the trouble of another phone call when you decide to try an all-grain brew.

2. Total alkalinity (carbonate/bicarbonate). This figure should be below 75 parts per million. Total alkalinity is often confused with pH, but they are not the same.

If you know a little about chemistry, you probably will recall that a high pH means "high alkalinity." However, these measures do not correlate very well. You cannot measure total alkalinity with a pH meter. Furthermore, municipal water can have a high pH but low total alkalinity. It is the total alkalinity of the water that matters, not the pH. That is why you need to get this information from a water chemist.

What if you have well water? In addition to problems of bacteria and iron content, which were discussed in Chapter 1 (see page 9), well water is often high in alkalinity. If your well water is all right for extract brewing — that is, low in iron — but you cannot have it analyzed, assume it has high total alkalinity and proceed accordingly.

The basic treatment for water in grain brewing is the same as for extract brewing: boil it. Boiling not only drives off chlorine and kills bacteria, it also removes most of the total alkalinity. The only catch is that you must boil all the water you brew with — about 8 gallons for a 5-gallon batch — for half an hour, *then* take the additional steps of letting the water cool (covered) overnight, and carefully racking it off into sanitized containers.

These steps are necessary because most of the alkalinity of water will precipitate as chalk, forming a "bathtub ring" around the inside of boiling kettle, and a fine, white, powdery deposit on the bottom. You must separate the water from these deposits, or they will redissolve when you make your wort.

Remember, you only need to do this if the total alkalinity of your water is over 75 parts per million. If it is lower, you can deal with your water just as you would when making extract beer.

THE SMALL-SCALE MASH METHOD

The first step is to crush all the grain malt called for in your recipe. This is easy to do with a Corona or other grain mill. Most homebrew supply shops will allow you to use their grain mill; some will even crush the grain for you. If you have been crushing your specialty malts with a champagne bottle, though, be warned that this method will not work with pale malt. You will have to use a mill.

Any experienced home brewer will be able to show you how to set up the mill for a proper crush. Basi-

Figure 3–2. Crushing the malt using a hand-cranked grain mill. Note the adjusting screw and the lock nut, which must be loosened before the adjusting screw can be turned.

shield (keeps dust from scattering)

lock nut

adjusting screw

cally, you want the coarsest setting that will break open the grains. The husks should remain in large pieces, and not be ground to powder.

After your malt is milled, the next step is to prepare your brewing water. This has been explained already. When the water is ready, measure your mash water into your smaller kettle. You should use 1⅓ quarts of water for every pound of grain. Heat the water to 163°F. and stir in the crushed malts. Maintain the temperature of the mash between 152° and 148°F. for 60 minutes. The easiest way to do this is to cover the kettle and put it on a rack in the oven, set at 140°F. Stir the mash several times during the course of this period.

During the mash period, all the grain starches will be converted into sugars. After this process is finished, the sweet wort must be strained off and the spent grains must be rinsed or *sparged* to recover all the sugar. The process goes as follows.

Sparging

While the mash is working, heat 2 gallons of prepared brewing water in your large kettle. The temperature should be between 160° and 168°F. At the end of the mashing process, stand or suspend your strainer over a 5-gallon bucket or other large container. Pour the mash into the strainer. Then transfer the hot sparge water to the mash kettle, and set it on the stove over very low heat to maintain its temperature.

Stand or suspend the strainer full

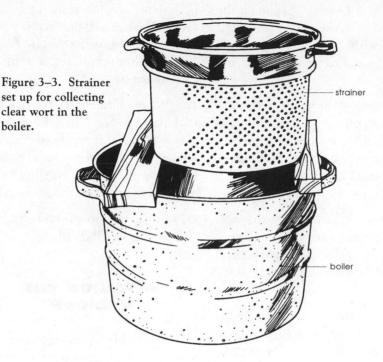

Figure 3–3. Strainer set up for collecting clear wort in the boiler.

strainer

boiler

of spent grains over the large brewing kettle. Then smooth out the surface and form a slight depression in the center of the grains with your spoon. Slowly pour the thick cloudy wort (collected in the bucket) through the spent grains to filter out most of the particles. Add about a quart at a time until all the wort has been put through the grain bed. Then begin adding sparge water, again about a quart at a time. Cover the entire surface of the grain bed. As soon as the water sinks below the top of the bed, add another quart.

When the last of the sparge water has been run through the grain bed filter, add the malt extract to the kettle. If using syrup, don't forget to rinse the container. Add prepared brewing water to bring the wort volume up to 6 gallons. Bring to a boil and boil for 1 hour total.

The rest of the partial-mash brewing process is the same as for the Advanced Extract Brewing Method, whose steps were explained in Chapter 2 and are repeated below.

SUMMARY OF THE PARTIAL-MASH BREWING METHOD

1. Prepare the yeast starter if necessary: 1 pint for ale yeasts, 1 quart for lager yeasts. Prepare the brewing water.

2. Crush the grains. Mash at 152° to 148°F. for 1 hour. Strain off the wort, recycle, then sparge the spent grains with 2 gallons of brewing water heated to between 160° and 168°F.

3. Dissolve the malt extracts in the wort, top up with brewing water to a total volume of 6 gallons, and bring the wort to a boil. Boil 1 hour total. During the boil, add hops as specified in the recipe.

4. Shut off heat. Cool the wort to the pitching temperature specified in the recipe. Strain or rack off whole hops (if used) into the starting tank.

5. Pitch the yeast starter or the amount of yeast slurry specified in the recipe. Aerate the wort thoroughly.

6. After 8 hours, carefully rack the beer into another fermenter, leaving behind the settled break material (trub). Affix airlock.

7. Allow the beer to ferment out.

7a. Optional, recommended with top-fermenting yeasts: Allow the beer to ferment until the kraeusen (yeasty foam head) reaches its peak and is just beginning to fall. Rack into another fermenter and allow to ferment out.

8. When fermentation is over, rack into a 5-gallon carboy and allow to settle for at least 5 days. Make up your priming sugar syrup. Rack the beer into a bottling tank and add the priming syrup. Bottle.

9. Store the bottles as directed in the recipe, in a dark place.

NOTES ON THE RECIPES

Some of the following recipes contain specifications which override the instructions given in the basic Partial-Mash Brewing Method: for example, they may call for a larger quantity of sparge water or a different mash temperature. In these cases, follow the specifics given in the recipe itself rather than the basic steps outlined above.

RECIPES

All recipes yield approximately 5 gallons (U.S.) of beer.

PALE ALE

Grains: 3 lbs. British pale ale malt; plus 8 oz. British crystal malt

Malt extract: 3.3 lbs. British pale syrup, unhopped

Bittering hops: 9 AAUs pellets or 11 AAUs whole hops — Fuggles, Goldings, or Northern Brewer

Finishing hops: 1.5 oz. Goldings

Yeast: Wyeast Labs #1028 or #1098, or M.eV. Research #9

Priming sugar: ½ cup corn sugar

Gravities: original gravity 1.044; terminal gravity 1.008–1.012

Brewer's Specifics

1. Add bittering hops 45 minutes before end of boil; add finishing hops 2 minutes before the end.
2. Pitching and fermentation temperature: 62–68°F.
3. Use 1 pint yeast starter or ½ cup slurry.
4. Isinglass finings may be added at bottling.
5. Store bottles 1 week at fermentation temperature, then 3 weeks at 50–60°F.

SCOTCH ALE

Grains: 3 lbs. British pale ale malt; plus 1 lb. British crystal malt; plus 4 oz. chocolate malt

Malt extract: 3.3 lbs. British pale syrup, unhopped

Sugar: 1 lb. dark brown sugar (add to wort)

Bittering hops: 7 AAUs pellets or 8 AAUs whole hops — Fuggles or Northern Brewer

Finishing hops: none

Yeast: Wyeast Labs #1098 or M.eV. Research #9

Priming sugar: ½ cup corn sugar

Gravities: original gravity 1.055; terminal gravity 1.010–1.014

Brewer's Specifics

1. Add bittering hops 45 minutes before end of boil.
2. Pitching and fermentation temperature: 62–68°F.
3. Use 1 pint yeast starter or ½ cup slurry.
4. Isinglass finings may be added at bottling.
5. Store bottles 1 week at fermentation temperature, then 3 weeks at 50–60°F.

LIGHT ALE

Grains: 3 lbs. British pale ale malt; plus 4 oz. British crystal malt
Malt extract: 1.5 lbs. British pale dry, unhopped
Bittering hops: 6 AAUs pellets or 8 AAUs whole hops — Fuggles, Goldings, or Northern Brewer
Finishing hops: ¾ oz. Goldings
Yeast: Wyeast Labs #1028 or #1098, or M.eV. Research #9
Priming sugar: ½ cup corn sugar
Gravities: original gravity 1.033; terminal gravity 1.005–1.007

Brewer's Specifics

1. Add bittering hops 45 minutes before end of boil; add finishing hops 2 minutes before the end.
2. Pitching and fermentation temperature: 62–68°F.
3. Use 1 pint yeast starter or ½ cup slurry.
4. Isinglass finings may be added at bottling.
5. Store bottles 1 week at fermentation temperature, then 3 weeks at 50–60°F.

BROWN ALE (MILD)

Grains: 2 lbs. British pale ale malt; plus 8 oz. British crystal malt; plus 4 oz. chocolate malt
Malt extract: 3.3 lbs. British pale syrup, unhopped
Sugar: 1 lb. dark brown sugar (add to wort)
Bittering hops: 5 AAUs pellets or 6 AAUs whole hops — Fuggles or Northern Brewer
Finishing hops: none
Yeast: Wyeast Labs #1028 or #1098, or M.eV. Research #9
Priming sugar: ½ cup corn sugar
Gravities: original gravity 1.045; terminal gravity 1.007–1.010

Brewer's Specifics

1. Add bittering hops 45 minutes before end of boil.
2. Pitching and fermentation temperature: 62–68°F.
3. Use 1 pint yeast starter or ½ cup slurry.
4. Isinglass finings may be added at bottling.
5. Store bottles 1 week at fermentation temperature, then 3 weeks at 50–60°F.

OLD ALE

Grains: 4 lbs. British pale ale malt; plus 1 lb. 60°L. crystal malt; plus 8 oz. chocolate malt

Malt extract: 3.3 lbs. British pale syrup, unhopped

Sugar: 24 oz. light molasses (add to wort)

Bittering hops: 7 AAUs pellets or 8 AAUs whole hops — Fuggles or Northern Brewer

Finishing hops: none

Yeast: Wyeast Labs #1098 or #1084, or M.eV. Research #9 or #4

Priming sugar: ½ cup corn sugar

Gravities: original gravity 1.063; terminal gravity 1.012–1.016

Brewer's Specifics

1. Use 2.5 gallons water to sparge.
2. Add bittering hops 45 minutes before end of boil.
3. Pitching and fermentation temperature: 62–68°F.
4. Use 1 pint yeast starter or ½ cup slurry.
5. Isinglass finings may be added at bottling.
6. Store bottles 1 week at fermentation temperature, then 6 weeks at 50–60°F.

PORTER

Grains: 3 lbs. British pale ale malt; plus 6 oz. roasted barley (crush each separately)

Malt extract: 3.3 lbs. British pale syrup, unhopped

Bittering hops: 8 AAUs pellets or 10 AAUs whole hops — Northern Brewer or other high-alpha British hops

Finishing hops: none

Yeast: Wyeast Labs #1028 or #1084, or M.eV. Research #4

Priming sugar: ½ cup corn sugar

Gravities: original gravity 1.044; terminal gravity 1.007–1.010

Brewer's Specifics

1. Stir the roasted barley into the mash 5 minutes before the end of the 1-hour mash period.
2. Add bittering hops 45 minutes before end of boil.
3. Pitching and fermentation temperature: 62–68°F.
4. Use 1 pint yeast starter or ½ cup slurry.
5. Isinglass finings may be added at bottling.
6. Store bottles 1 week at fermentation temperature, then 3 weeks at 50–60°F.

DRY STOUT

Grains: 3 lbs. British pale ale malt; plus 8 oz. flaked barley malt, added as adjunct to the mash kettle; plus 12 oz. roasted barley (crush each separately)

Malt extract: 3.3 lbs. British pale syrup, unhopped

Bittering hops: 10 AAUs pellets or 12 AAUs whole hops — Northern Brewer or other high-alpha British hops

Finishing hops: none

Yeast: Wyeast Labs #1028 or #1084, or M.eV. Research #4

Priming sugar: ½ cup corn sugar

Gravities: original gravity 1.046; terminal gravity 1.008–1.012

Brewer's Specifics

1. Stir the roasted barley into the mash 5 minutes before the end of the 1-hour mash period.
2. Add bittering hops 45 minutes before end of boil.
3. Pitching and fermentation temperature: 62–68°F.
4. Use 1 pint yeast starter or ½ cup slurry.
5. Isinglass finings may be added at bottling.
6. Store bottles 1 week at fermentation temperature, then 3 weeks at 50–60°F.

SWEET STOUT

Grains: 3 lbs. British pale ale malt; plus 8 oz. British crystal malt; plus 6 oz. roasted barley (crush each separately)

Malt extract: 3.3 lbs. British pale syrup, unhopped

Bittering hops: 7 AAUs pellets or 8 AAUs whole hops — Northern Brewer or other high-alpha British hops

Finishing hops: none

Yeast: Wyeast Labs #1028 or #1084, or M.eV. Research #4

Priming sugar: ½ cup corn sugar

Gravities: original gravity 1.045; terminal gravity 1.008–1.012

Brewer's Specifics

1. Stir the roasted barley into the mash 5 minutes before the end of the 1-hour mash period.
2. Add bittering hops 45 minutes before end of boil.
3. Pitching and fermentation temperature: 62–68°F.
4. Use 1 pint yeast starter or ½ cup slurry.
5. Isinglass finings may be added at bottling.
6. Store bottles 1 week at fermentation temperature, then 3 weeks at 50–60°F.

IMPERIAL STOUT

Grains: 4 lbs. British pale ale malt; plus 1 lb. British crystal malt; plus 4 oz. chocolate malt; plus 4 oz. roasted barley (crush each separately)

Malt extract: 6.6 lbs. British dark syrup, unhopped

Sugar: 1 lb. dark brown sugar (add to wort)

Bittering hops: 10 AAUs pellets or 12 AAUs whole hops — Northern Brewer or other high-alpha British hops

Finishing hops: none

Yeast: Wyeast Labs #1056 or #1084, or M.eV. Research #72 or #4

Priming sugar: ½ cup corn syrup

Gravities: original gravity 1.086; terminal gravity 1.017–1.024

Brewer's Specifics

1. Stir the roasted barley into the mash 5 minutes before the end of the 1-hour mash period.
2. Use 2.5 gallons water to sparge.
3. Add bittering hops 45 minutes before end of boil.
4. Pitching and fermentation temperature: 62–68°F.
5. Use 1 pint yeast starter or ½ cup slurry. (Note: If fermentation hangs, the yeast may have been killed by the high alcohol content. Rack off, add 1 teaspoon yeast nutrient, and repitch with a packet of rehydrated champagne yeast.)
6. Isinglass finings may be added at bottling.
7. Store bottles 2 weeks at fermentation temperature, then 12 weeks at 50–60°F.

BARLEY WINE

Grains: 4 lbs. British pale ale malt; plus 12 oz. British crystal malt

Malt extract: 6.6 lbs. British pale syrup, unhopped

Sugar: 1.5 lbs. light brown or raw sugar (add to wort)

Bittering hops: 13 AAUs pellets or 15 AAUs whole hops — Fuggles, Goldings, or Northern Brewer

Finishing hops: none

Yeast: Wyeast Labs #1028 or #1056, or M.eV. Research #72

Priming sugar: ½ cup corn sugar

Gravities: original gravity 1.086; terminal gravity 1.017–1.023

Brewer's Specifics

1. Use 2.5 gallons water to sparge.
2. Add bittering hops 45 minutes before end of boil.
3. Pitching and fermentation temperature: 62–68°F.
4. Use 1 pint yeast starter or ½ cup slurry. (Note: If fermentation hangs, the yeast may have been killed by the high alcohol content. Rack off, add 1 teaspoon yeast nutrient, then repitch with a packet of rehydrated champagne yeast.)
5. Isinglass finings may be added at bottling.
6. Store bottles 2 weeks at fermentation temperature, then 12 weeks at 50–60°F.

ALTBIER

Grains: 3.5 lbs. pale 2-row malt; plus 8 oz. 40°L. crystal malt; plus 1 oz. black malt

Malt extract: 3.3 lbs. Northwestern Weizen syrup, unhopped

Bittering hops: 8 AAUs pellets or 10 AAUs whole hops — Hallertau, Tettnanger, Spalt, or Perle

Finishing hops: none

Yeast: Wyeast Labs #1007 or #1338, or M.eV. Research #3

Priming sugar: ¾ cup corn syrup

Gravities: original gravity 1.046; terminal gravity 1.008–1.012

Brewer's Specifics

1. Add two-thirds of bittering hops 45 minutes before end of boil; add remaining third 15 minutes before the end.
2. Pitching and fermentation temperature: 62–68°F.
3. Use 1 pint yeast starter or ½ cup slurry.
4. Isinglass finings may be added at bottling.
5. Store bottles 1 week at fermentation temperature, then 3 weeks at 40–50°F.

KOLSCH

Grains: 2 lbs. pale 2-row malt; plus 8 oz. Vienna malt
Malt extract: 4 lbs. Alexander's pale syrup, unhopped
Bittering hops: 5 AAUs pellets or 6 AAUs whole hops — Hallertau,
   Tettnanger, Spalt, or Perle
Finishing hops: none
Yeast: Wyeast Labs #1007 or #1338, or M.eV. Research #3
Priming sugar: ¾ cup corn sugar
Gravities: original gravity 1.044; terminal gravity 1.006–1.009

Brewer's Specifics

1. Add two-thirds of bittering hops 45 minutes before end of boil; add
    remaining third 15 minutes before the end.
2. Pitching and fermentation temperature: 62–68°F.
3. Use 1 pint yeast starter or ½ cup slurry.
4. Isinglass finings may be added at bottling.
5. Store bottles 1 week at fermentation temperature, then 3 weeks at 40–
    50°F.

WEISSBIER

Grains: 2.5 lbs. pale 2-row malt
Malt extract: 2 lbs. Briess Weizen dry, unhopped
Bittering hops: 3.5 AAUs pellets or 4 AAUs whole hops — Hallertau,
   Tettnanger, Spalt, or Perle
Finishing hops: none
Yeast: Wyeast Labs #1007 or #1338, or M.eV. Research #3
Priming sugar: 1 cup corn sugar
Gravities: original gravity 1.034; terminal gravity about 1.005

Brewer's Specifics

1. Add two-thirds of bittering hops 45 minutes before end of boil; add remaining third 15 minutes before the end.
2. Pitching and fermentation temperature: 62–68°F.
3. Use 1 pint yeast starter or ½ cup slurry.
4. Isinglass finings may be added at bottling. Lactic acid may also be added to taste if the tartness of authentic Berliner Weissbier is desired.
5. Store bottles 1 week at fermentation temperature, then 3 weeks at 50–60°F.

WEIZEN

Grains: 2 lbs. pale 2-row malt; plus 1 lb. wheat malt (crush finer than barley malt)
Malt extract: 3 lbs. Briess Weizen dry, unhopped
Bittering hops: 5 AAUs pellets or 6 AAUs whole hops — Hallertau, Tettnanger, Spalt, or Perle
Finishing hops: none
Yeast: Wyeast Labs #3056 or M.eV. Research #33
Priming sugar: 1 cup corn sugar
Gravities: original gravity 1.048; terminal gravity 1.008–1.012

Brewer's Specifics

1. Add two-thirds of bittering hops 45 minutes before end of boil; add remaining third 15 minutes before the end.
2. Pitching and fermentation temperature: 62–68°F.
3. Use 1 pint yeast starter or ½ cup slurry.
4. Isinglass finings may be added at bottling.
5. Store bottles 1 week at fermentation temperature, then 3 weeks at 50–60°F.

WIT

Grains: 3 lbs. pale 2-row malt
Malt extract: 3.3 lbs. Northwestern Weizen syrup, unhopped
Bittering hops: 4 AAUs pellets or 5 AAUs whole hops — Hallertau, Fuggles, or Goldings
Finishing hops: none
Yeast: Wyeast Labs #1007 or #1338, or M.eV. Research #3
Special ingredient: 1 oz. coriander seed
Priming sugar: ¾ cup corn sugar
Gravities: original gravity 1.043; terminal gravity 1.006–1.008

Brewer's Specifics

1. Add two-thirds of bittering hops 45 minutes before end of boil; add remaining third 15 minutes before the end.
2. Pitching and fermentation temperature: 62–68°F.
3. Use 1 pint yeast starter or ½ cup slurry.
4. Crush coriander seeds and put into a 5-gallon carboy just before racking. Allow to sit 2 weeks before bottling.
5. Isinglass finings may be added at bottling.
6. Store bottles 1 week at fermentation temperature, then 3 weeks at 50–60°F.

TRAPPIST ALE

Grains: 3 lbs. pale 2-row malt; plus 8 oz. 40°L. crystal malt
Malt extract: 6 lbs. British amber dry, unhopped
Sugar: 1 lb. dark brown sugar (add to wort)
Bittering hops: 9 AAUs pellets or 11 AAUs whole hops — Hallertau and Fuggles (50–50 blend)
Finishing hops: none
Yeast: Fresh culture from a Chimay ale bottle
Priming sugar: ½ cup corn sugar
Gravities: original gravity 1.075; terminal gravity 1.015–1.020

Brewer's Specifics

1. Add two-thirds of bittering hops 45 minutes before end of boil; add remaining third 15 minutes before the end.
2. Pitching and fermentation temperature: 70–75°F.
3. Use 1 quart yeast starter (follow the two-step culture process described on page 36).
4. Isinglass finings may be added at bottling.
5. Store bottles 2 weeks at fermentation temperature, then 8 weeks at 50–60°F.

CREAM ALE

Grains: 2 lbs. pale 6-row malt; plus 1 lb. flaked maize (corn)
Malt extract: 3.3 lbs. Northwestern pale syrup, unhopped
Bittering hops: 4 AAUs pellets or 5 AAUs whole hops — Hallertau, Tettnanger, Perle, or Cascade
Finishing hops: ½ oz. Tettnanger or Cascade
Yeast: Wyeast Labs #1056 or M.eV. Research #69
Priming sugar: ¾ cup corn sugar
Gravities: original gravity 1.044; terminal gravity 1.006–1.008

Brewer's Specifics

1. Add bittering hops 45 minutes before end of boil. Add whole finishing hops 5 minutes before the end, pellet finishing hops at the end of the boil.
2. Pitching and fermentation temperature: 62–68°F.
3. Use 1 pint yeast starter or ½ cup slurry.
4. Isinglass finings may be added at bottling.
5. Store bottles 1 week at fermentation temperature, then 4 weeks at 40–50°F.

FRUIT ALE

Grain: 3 lbs. pale 2-row malt
Malt extract: 3 lbs. Briess Weizen dry, unhopped
Bittering hops: 1.5 AAUs pellets or 2 AAUs whole hops — any type
Finishing hops: none
Special ingredient: 10 lbs. cherries, raspberries, or peaches, washed and crushed (used in second fermentation)
Yeast: Wyeast Labs #1007 or #1338, or M.eV. Research #3
Priming sugar: 1¼ cups corn sugar
Gravities: original gravity 1.047; terminal gravity 1.008–1.012

Brewer's Specifics

1. Add all hops 45 minutes before end of boil.
2. Pitching and fermentation temperature: 62–68°F.
3. Use 1 pint yeast starter or ½ cup slurry.
4. After 1 week of fermentation, add the freshly prepared fruit to a second fermenter and rack the beer over it. Allow to ferment for 4 weeks before racking off into the 5-gallon carboy.
5. Isinglass finings may be added at bottling.
6. Store bottles 1 week at fermentation temperature, then 6 weeks at 40–50°F.

CALIFORNIA COMMON BEER

Grains: 3.5 lbs. pale 2-row malt; plus 8 oz. 40°L. crystal malt
Malt extract: 3.3 lbs. Northwestern pale syrup, unhopped
Bittering hops: 10 AAUs pellets or 12 AAUs whole hops — Northern Brewer or Cascade
Finishing hops: 1.5 oz. Northern Brewer or Cascade
Yeast: Wyeast Labs #2007 or M.eV. Research #4
Priming sugar: ¾ cup corn sugar
Gravities: original gravity 1.045; terminal gravity 1.007–1.012

Brewer's Specifics

1. Add bittering hops 45 minutes before end of boil. Add whole finishing hops 5 minutes before the end, pellet finishing hops at the end of the boil.

2. Pitching and fermentation temperature: 62–68°F.

3. Use 1 quart yeast starter or ⅔ cup slurry.

4. Store bottles 1 week at fermentation temperature, then 4 weeks at temperatures as cool as possible (32°F. minimum).

LIGHT-BODIED PILSNER

Grains: 1.5 lbs. pale 6-row malt; plus 1 lb. flaked maize (corn)

Malt extract: 4 lbs. Alexander's pale syrup, unhopped

Bittering hops: 3.5 AAUs pellets or 4 AAUs whole hops — Hallertau, Tettnanger, or Cascade

Finishing hops: ½ oz. Tettnanger, Cascade, or Saaz

Yeast: Wyeast Labs #2007 or #2042, or M.eV. Research #4 or #55

Priming sugar: ¾ cup corn sugar

Gravities: original gravity 1.043; terminal gravity 1.006–1.010.

Brewer's Specifics

1. Add two-thirds of bittering hops 45 minutes before end of boil; add remaining third 15 minutes before end. Add whole finishing hops 5 minutes before the end, pellet finishing hops at the end of the boil. (Note: For a European flavor, increase bittering hops to 5–7 AAUs and use Saaz finishing hops.)

2. Pitching and fermentation temperature: 50–55°F.

3. Use 1 quart yeast starter or ⅔ cup slurry.

4. Store bottles 10 days at fermentation temperature, then 4 weeks at temperatures as cool as possible (32°F. minimum).

CLASSIC ALL-MALT PILSNER

Grains: 3 lbs. 2-row pale malt; plus 8 oz. dextrin (Cara-pils) malt
Malt extract: 4 lbs. Alexander's pale syrup, unhopped
Bittering hops: 7–9 AAUs pellets or 9–11 AAUs whole hops — Hallertau,
    Tettnanger, or Cascade
Finishing hops: 1–1.5 oz. Saaz
Yeast: Wyeast Labs #2124, #2042, or #2308, or M.eV. Research #55 or #37
Priming sugar: ¾ cup corn sugar
Gravities: original gravity 1.050; terminal gravity 1.007–1.011

Brewer's Specifics

1. Add two-thirds of bittering hops 45 minutes before end of boil; add
    remaining third 15 minutes before end. Add whole finishing hops 5
    minutes before the end, pellet finishing hops at the end of the boil.
2. Pitching and fermentation temperature: 46–50°F.
3. Use 1 quart yeast starter or ⅔ cup slurry.
4. Store bottles 10 days at fermentation temperature, then 4 weeks at
    temperatures as cool as possible (32°F. minimum).

MUNICH HELLES

Grains: 2 lbs. pale 2-row malt; plus 8 oz. Vienna malt; plus 8 oz. dextrin
    (Cara-pils) malt
Malt extract: 3 lbs. Briess pale dry, unhopped
Bittering hops: 5 AAUs pellets or 6 AAUs whole hops — Hallertau,
    Tettnanger, Perle, or Mt. Hood
Finishing hops: ¼ oz. Tettnanger or Hallertau
Yeast: Wyeast Labs #2206 or #2308, or M.eV. Research #37
Priming sugar: ¾ cup corn sugar
Gravities: original gravity 1.046; terminal gravity 1.007–1.011

Brewer's Specifics

1. Add two-thirds of bittering hops 45 minutes before end of boil; add remaining third 15 minutes before end. Add whole finishing hops 5 minutes before the end, pellet finishing hops at the end of the boil.
2. Pitching and fermentation temperature: 46–50°F.
3. Use 1 quart yeast starter or ⅔ cup slurry.
4. Store bottles 10 days at fermentation temperature, then 4 weeks at temperatures as cool as possible (32°F. minimum).

MUNICH DUNKEL

Grains: 1 lb. pale 2-row malt; plus 2.5 lbs. Munich malt; plus 8 oz. 60°L. crystal malt; plus 1 oz. black malt

Malt extract: 3 lbs. Briess pale dry, unhopped

Bittering hops: 5 AAUs pellets or 6 AAUs whole hops — Hallertau, Tettnanger, Perle, or Mt. Hood

Finishing hops: none

Yeast: Wyeast Labs #2206 or #2308, or M.eV. Research #37

Priming sugar: ¾ cup corn sugar

Gravities: original gravity 1.050; terminal gravity 1.010–1.014

Brewer's Specifics

1. Add two-thirds of bittering hops 45 minutes before end of boil, add remaining third 15 minutes before end.
2. Pitching and fermentation temperature: 46–50°F.
3. Use 1 quart yeast starter or ⅔ cup slurry.
4. Store bottles 10 days at fermentation temperature, then 4 weeks at temperatures as cool as possible (32°F. minimum).

DORTMUNDER EXPORT

Grains: 2 lbs. pale 2-row malt; plus 8 oz. Vienna malt; plus 8 oz. dextrin (Cara-pils) malt

Malt extract: 4 lbs. Briess pale dry, unhopped

Bittering hops: 6 AAUs pellets or 7 AAUs whole hops — Hallertau, Tettnanger, Perle, or Mt. Hood

Finishing hops: ½ oz. Tettnanger or Hallertau

Yeast: Wyeast Labs #2206 or #2308, or M.eV. Research #37

Priming sugar: ¾ cup corn sugar

Gravities: original gravity 1.056; terminal gravity 1.011–1.015

Brewer's Specifics

1. Add two-thirds of bittering hops 45 minutes before end of boil; add remaining third 15 minutes before end. Add whole finishing hops 5 minutes before the end, pellet finishing hops at the end of the boil.
2. Pitching and fermentation temperature: 46–50°F.
3. Use 1 quart yeast starter or ⅔ cup slurry.
4. Store bottles 10 days at fermentation temperature, then 5 weeks at temperatures as cool as possible (32°F. minimum).

OKTOBERFEST (MÄRZEN)

Grains: 1 lb. pale 2-row malt; plus 2.5 lbs. Munich malt; plus 4 oz. 40°L. crystal malt

Malt extract: 3 lbs. Briess pale dry, unhopped; plus 1 lb. Briess amber dry, unhopped

Bittering hops: 6 AAUs pellets or 7 AAUs whole hops — Hallertau, Tettnanger, Perle, or Mt. Hood

Finishing hops: none

Yeast: Wyeast Labs #2206 or #2308, or M.eV. Research #37

Priming sugar: ¾ cup corn sugar

Gravities: original gravity 1.056; terminal gravity 1.012–1.016

Brewer's Specifics

1. Add two-thirds of bittering hops 45 minutes before end of boil; add remaining third 15 minutes before end.
2. Pitching and fermentation temperature: 46–50°F.
3. Use 1 quart yeast starter or ⅔ cup slurry.
4. Store bottles 10 days at fermentation temperature, then 5 weeks at temperatures as cool as possible (32°F. minimum).

HELLES BOCK

Grains: 2 lbs. pale 2-row malt; plus 1 lb. Vienna malt; plus 1 lb. dextrin (Cara-pils) malt

Malt extract: 4 lbs. Alexander's pale syrup, unhopped; plus 1 lb. Briess pale dry, unhopped

Bittering hops: 7 AAUs pellets or 8 AAUs whole hops — Hallertau, Tettnanger, Perle, or Mt. Hood

Finishing hops: ¼ oz. Tettnanger or Hallertau

Yeast: Wyeast Labs #2206 or #2308, or M.eV. Research #37

Priming sugar: ¾ cup corn sugar

Gravities: original gravity 1.066; terminal gravity 1.014–1.018

Brewer's Specifics

1. Use 2.5 gallons water to sparge.
2. Add two-thirds of bittering hops 45 minutes before end of boil; add remaining third 15 minutes before end. Add whole finishing hops 5 minutes before the end, pellet finishing hops at the end of the boil.
3. Pitching and fermentation temperature: 46–50°F.
4. Use 1 quart yeast starter or ⅔ cup slurry.
5. Store bottles 10 days at fermentation temperature, then 6 weeks at temperatures as cool as possible (32°F. minimum).

DUNKEL BOCK

Grains: 1 lb. pale 2-row malt; plus 2 lbs. Munich malt; plus 1.5 lbs. 60°L. crystal malt

Malt extract: 3 lbs. Briess amber dry, unhopped; plus 1.5 lbs. Briess pale dry, unhopped

Bittering hops: 7 AAUs pellets or 8 AAUs whole hops — Hallertau, Tettnanger, Perle, or Mt. Hood

Finishing hops: none

Yeast: Wyeast Labs #2206 or #2308, or M.eV. Research #37

Priming sugar: ¾ cup corn sugar

Gravities: original gravity 1.065; terminal gravity 1.016–1.020

Brewer's Specifics

1. Use 2.5 gallons water to sparge.
2. Add two-thirds of bittering hops 45 minutes before end of boil; add remaining third 15 minutes before end.
3. Pitching and fermentation temperature: 46–50°F.
4. Use 1 quart yeast starter or ⅔ cup slurry.
5. Store bottles 10 days at fermentation temperature, then 6 weeks at temperatures as cool as possible (32°F. minimum).

DOPPELBOCK

Follow the recipe above, but increase the pale dry malt extract to 2.5 lbs. Original gravity will be about 1.075, terminal gravity about 1.020.

THE LAST STEP: ALL-GRAIN BREWING

All-grain brewing is only a little more complex and time-consuming than partial-mash brewing. The main difference between the two is the mind-set required. When you make a partial mash, most of the fermentable sugar in your wort is derived from malt extract. Even if you somehow muff the mash, you are still going to end up with a batch of beer at the end of the day.

The challenge of all-grain brewing is to cut loose from that reassurance. Going to a full mash means working without a net. On the other hand, if you have done a partial mash, you already know that the process works. Crush some malt, make up a porridge with it, let it rest for an hour or so at 150°F., and the grain starch will change to sugar. It's almost automatic.

EQUIPMENT

There are only three pieces of equipment you really need to become a full-mash brewer, in addition to the kit you have already assembled.

Grain Mill

You already know how to use a mill. I strongly suggest that when you get into all-grain brewing you buy one for yourself. It is much more convenient to have one at home, permanently mounted on a bench or stand where it is always ready to use. Also, you can modify it by installing a shaft that holds a drive pulley, or fits in the chuck of a high-torque drill. Motorizing your grain mill will eliminate 80 percent of the aggravation of grain brewing.

Lauter Tun

The simplest design is the one pictured in Figure 4–1 on the next page. You will notice that, if you already made a strainer out of a 4-gallon bucket for partial mashes, all you need to do is cut a hole in a 5-gallon bucket and install a plastic spigot as shown.

The lauter tun makes it possible to run off clean wort into the boiling kettle, and to regulate the flow so that you recover all the malt sugar from your mash.

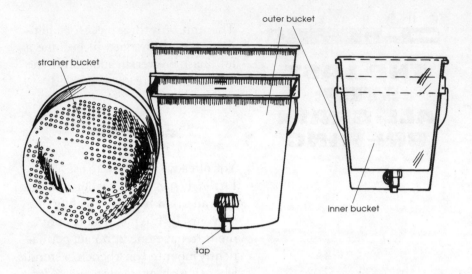

Figure 4–1. A lauter tun made from two food-grade plastic buckets.

pH Measurement Strips

When I talked about water in Chapter 3, I said that the pH of the brewing water is not important. That's true. What I did not say is that the pH of the mash *is* important. Under normal conditions, with good (low-alkalinity) brewing water, the pH of the mash will be fine. However, when your whole brew is on the line, it is wise to check it just to be sure. Mash pH is easy to adjust if necessary. In addition, you will get better brewing results if you adjust the pH of your sparge water as the commercial breweries do. This makes little difference with a partial mash, but, again, it becomes more significant with all-grain brews.

The best pH measurement strips are those made by Merck and sold under the brand name ColorpHast. They are thin strips of plastic coated with indicator compound on one end. You need the strips that cover the range from pH 4.0 to 7.0. Always be sure to let your sample (mash or water) cool to room temperature before dipping the strip into it. Read the strip carefully and in good light. Always discard samples after reading them.

An alternative to strips are pH meters, which are easier to read. If you decide to spring for one, make sure it can be calibrated and that it has a replaceable electrode.

MATERIALS

The basic materials are the same for all-grain as for partial-mash brewing. The additional materials discussed here are minor components that will help in getting optimum results.

pH Adjustment Compounds

These fall into two distinct classes: *calcium salts*, which are used to adjust the pH of the mash; and *acids*, which are used to adjust the pH of the sparge water.

Two different calcium salts can be used to *lower* the pH of the mash: gypsum (calcium sulfate) and calcium chloride. I prefer gypsum for pale ales, calcium chloride for lagers. To *raise* the mash pH, calcium carbonate is the only choice. All three of these compounds are available at homebrew supply stores. If

you use any other source, be doubly certain you are buying food-grade or USP (pharmaceutical-grade) material. This warning also applies to the acids used for adjusting mash water. Any acid will lower the pH of sparge water, but many have undesirable flavors. Phosphoric acid is arguably the best, but sulfuric, hydrochloric, and lactic acid can also be used. If the acid is highly concentrated (for example, 88 percent lactic acid), you should dilute it with 9 parts water or more and use this dilute stock to adjust the pH of your sparge water.

Clarifying Agents

You have already been introduced to isinglass, which is used to counteract yeast haze. All-grain beers are

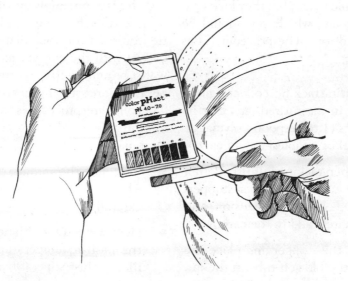

Figure 4-2. Reading the pH of the mash.

prone to hazes caused by natural compounds (proteins and polyphenols) derived from the malt. Beer clarifiers remove some of these compounds and are the only way to knock out *chill haze* (which forms when beer is refrigerated) without using a filter.

Polyclar is a synthetic plastic compound, ground into a fine powder. *Silica gel* is similar in appearance. Both these compounds are available at homebrew supply stores. *Bentonite* is a possible substitute for silica gel, but it is much more difficult to use, so I would avoid it. These compounds work best when used together, especially for pale beers. I suggest 1 tablespoon of each for a 5-gallon batch. If the finished beer still throws a chill haze, you can double this dosage on the next brew.

Clarifiers are added during racking, after fermentation is over. They are simple to use, but they kick up a lot of foam, which you should be prepared for. The procedure is as follows:

1. During racking, collect 1 quart of beer in a sanitized jar. Stir in clarifiers (1 tablespoon Polyclar or silica gel or 1 tablespoon of each).

2. When racking is finished, fit a blowoff tube to a rubber stopper. Stir the clarifier suspension and immediately add to the carboy.

3. Fit the stopper and place the end of the blowoff tube in the jar. Replace with an airlock when the foaming ends.

Subsequent steps are the same as for any other beer.

MASHING, LAUTERING, AND SPARGING TECHNIQUES

As an all-grain brewer, you need to be familiar with the basic steps involved in the mash process and the subsequent collection of the sweet wort. You should also learn a little of the brewers' terminology used to describe them.

Mashing In

Mashing in means mixing the crushed malt and any adjuncts with a predetermined amount of water (1⅓ quarts per pound). In home brewing, this is done simply by filling the mash kettle (the same 5-gallon kettle you used for your first extract brews) with the correct amount of water, bringing it to the correct temperature, and stirring in the grain. The following procedures and information are crucial to the success of your mash.

■ Calculate the amount of mash water needed and measure it carefully.

■ Heat water 11°F. higher than the mash-in temperature specified in the recipe. On mixing, the mash will then be at or near the temperature specified.

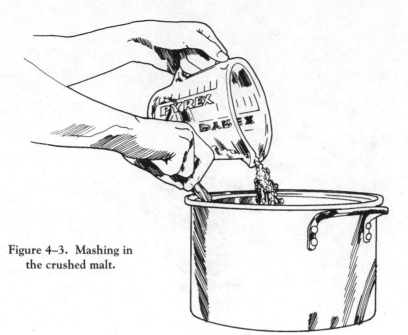

Figure 4–3. Mashing in
the crushed malt.

■ Mash temperature is important, as higher or lower temperatures can affect the terminal gravity and mouthfeel (body) of the finished beer. High temperatures result in a high terminal gravity, whereas low temperatures do just the opposite. Generally, a temperature deviation of 2°F. will make a noticeable difference. Smaller differences can be ignored.

■ If necessary, adjust the mash temperature by applying heat for a minute at a time, while stirring vigorously. To lower the temperature, stir in a pint or two of cold water.

■ As soon as the temperature is set, check the mash pH. Any reading between 5.0 and 5.7 is fine. If it is higher, add ½ teaspoon of gypsum or calcium chloride and stir it in for 2 minutes before checking again. Repeat if necessary. If the pH is too low, follow the same procedure as above, but add calcium carbonate.

Mashing

Mashing itself is just a matter of allowing the malt enzymes to convert all the grain starches to sugar.

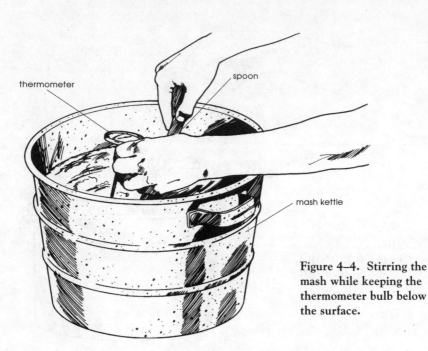

thermometer

spoon

mash kettle

Figure 4–4. Stirring the mash while keeping the thermometer bulb below the surface.

■ Maintain the mash temperature just as with a partial mash, by setting the kettle, covered, in a 140°F. oven. Stir several times during the mash period. If the mash temperature drops a few degrees during this period, it is not important. The critical specification is the *starting* temperature.

■ Some recipes suggest a multi-temperature mash. This will give you a clearer wort (and beer), but it is always optional. If you want to use this procedure, the best way to boost the mash temperature is to apply full heat for a few minutes at a time, stirring vigorously. Shut off the heat between bursts and stir for 1 minute with the thermometer in the mash before reading the temperature. Always read the thermometer with the bulb or stem in the center of the kettle, halfway down. As you approach the temperature for the next rest, cut down the time of your heat bursts in order to avoid an overshoot.

The Mash-Out

The *mash-out* is an optional step in which the mash temperature is boosted to 168°F. and held there for 5 minutes before the mash is transferred to the lauter tun. The wort runs off faster at the higher temperature. If you wish to include this step, follow the instructions above for boosting the temperature.

■ You will be sparging your mash with 5 gallons of fairly hot water. To avoid delays, heat this water in your boiling kettle during the last 30 to 45 minutes of the mash period.

■ It is best to figure out how much acid you must add to adjust your sparge water in advance. You want to lower its pH to between 5.7 and 5.5. Experiment with a gallon of water, using your stock solution of acid. Multiply the required amount by the volume (in gallons) of sparge water needed — usually 5.

Lautering and Sparging the Wort

When the mash period is over, it is time to run off the sweet wort and sparge the spent grains. Basically, you use the grains as a filter bed to clarify the wort. Then you rinse the bed with hot water to recover the sugar trapped within it.

The first step is to transfer the mash from the kettle to the lauter tun. (Double check to make sure the spigot is closed before you do this.) Then set the lauter tun on a tabletop with the spigot hanging over the edge. Tilt the lauter tun by placing a book under one end (see Fig. 4–5). Cover the tun and let the mash sit for a few minutes. Pour most of your sparge water into the mash kettle, then set it on the stove.

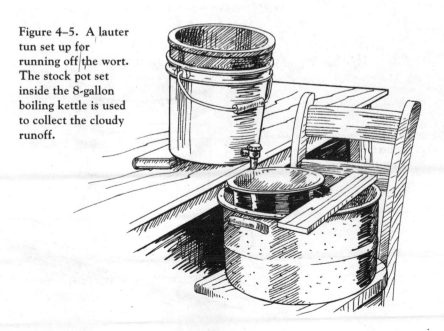

Figure 4–5. A lauter tun set up for running off the wort. The stock pot set inside the 8-gallon boiling kettle is used to collect the cloudy runoff.

Set the burner on low heat to maintain the temperature of the water at 160–168°F. — no higher. Add the remaining sparge water to the mash kettle, then set the larger boiling kettle on a chair beneath the spigot of the lauter tun. Set or suspend a stock pot (6-quart or larger) inside the boiler to collect the cloudy wort.

Now, open the spigot wide and let the wort run off. As it does so, the level of liquid in the lauter tun will sink and the flow will slow down. Eventually, the wort will drop below the surface of the grain bed. When this happens, level off the surface with your spoon and add a quart of cloudy wort back to the lauter tun. (A 1-quart Pyrex measuring cup is ideal for this.)

Continue to recirculate the sweet wort until the runoff is clear. Wort will never become crystal clear like a commercial beer, but it should appear bright, with only a slight haze apparent when you hold a wineglassful up to the light. When this happens, remove the stock pot and let the wort run into the boiling kettle. Put the stock pot on the stove over low heat and continue to add the cloudy wort, 1 quart at a time, until all the cloudy runoff has been filtered through the grain bed.

Some spigots are prone to clogging. If this happens when you start running off the wort, remove the handle and internal mechanism. Replace them when the outflow has slowed down.

Figure 4–6. Continue to recirculate the cloudy wort through the grain bed in the lauter tun until the runoff is clear.

Sparge the grain bed with the hot sparge water, adding 2 quarts at a time. The total time to put 5 gallons of sparge water through the grain bed should not be less than 45 minutes. If necessary, restrict the outflow by partly closing the spigot. A rapid sparge will not retrieve all the malt sugar from the spent grains.

After adding all the sparge water, allow 10 to 15 minutes for the filter bed to drain before closing the spigot and putting the kettle on the stove. Stir the wort, because the heavy first runnings tend to scorch on the bottom of the kettle.

The remainder of the brewing process is the same as with partial-mash or advanced malt-extract brewing. The only difference between the three methods, really, is the way you make up the wort. The summary given below confirms this.

SUMMARY OF THE FULL-MASH BREWING METHOD

1. Prepare the yeast starter if necessary: 1 pint for ale yeasts, 1 quart for lager yeasts. Prepare the brewing water.

2. Crush the grains. Heat the mash water to 11°F. over the mash temperature specified in the recipe. Stir the grains in and mix thoroughly. Check the mash temperature and apply heat if necessary to raise the mash to the temperature specified in the recipe.

Adjust the pH if necessary. Set the mash rest(s) for the specific time(s) and temperature(s) called for in the recipe.

3. Optional: Boost mash temperature to 165–168°F. and let stand for 5 minutes.

4. Transfer the mash to the lauter tun, run off the wort, and recirculate until clear. Then sparge the spent grains with 5 gallons water at 160–168°F.

5. Stir the wort and bring it to a boil over full heat. Boil the wort for 75 minutes total, adding the hops as called for in the recipe. Adjust boiling rate so as to finish with 5¼ gallons of wort.

6. Shut off heat. Cool the wort to the pitching temperature specified in the recipe. Strain or rack off whole hops (if used) into the starting tank.

7. Pitch the yeast starter or the amount of yeast slurry specified in the recipe. Aerate the wort thoroughly.

8. After 8 hours, carefully rack the beer into another fermenter, leaving behind the settled break material (trub). Affix airlock.

9. Allow the beer to ferment out.

9a. Optional, recommended with top-fermenting yeasts: Allow the beer to ferment until the kraeusen (yeasty foam head) reaches its peak and is just beginning to fall. Rack into another fermenter and allow to ferment out.

10. When fermentation is over, rack into a 5-gallon carboy, adding clarifiers if desired. Allow to settle for at least 5 days. Make up your priming sugar syrup. Rack the beer into a bottling tank and add the priming syrup. Bottle. Store the bottles as directed in the recipe, in a dark place.

RECIPES

All recipes yield approximately 5 gallons (U.S.) of beer.

PALE ALE

Grains: 7 lbs. British pale ale malt; plus 8 oz. British crystal malt
Bittering hops: 9 AAUs pellets or 11 AAUs whole hops — Fuggles, Goldings, or Northern Brewer
Finishing hops: 1.5 oz. Goldings
Yeast: Wyeast Labs #1028 or #1098, or M.eV. Research #9
Priming sugar: ½ cup corn sugar or ⅓ cup firmly packed dark brown sugar
Gravities: original gravity 1.048; terminal gravity 1.010–1.014

Brewer's Specifics

1. Mash temperature: 150°F. at start. Mash time: 2 hours
2. Add bittering hops 45 minutes before end of boil; add finishing hops 2 minutes before the end.
3. Pitching and fermentation temperature: 62–68°F.
4. Use 1 pint yeast starter or ½ cup slurry.
5. Isinglass finings may be added at bottling.
6. Store bottles 1 week at fermentation temperature, then 3 weeks at 50–60°F.

LIGHT ALE

Grains: 4.5 lbs. British pale ale malt; plus 4 oz. British crystal malt; plus 8 oz. flaked maize (corn)
Bittering hops: 6 AAUs pellets or 7 AAUs whole hops — Fuggles, Goldings, or Northern Brewer
Finishing hops: ½ oz. Goldings
Yeast: Wyeast Labs #1028 or #1098, or M.eV. Research #9
Priming sugar: ½ cup corn sugar or ⅓ cup firmly packed dark brown sugar
Gravities: original gravity 1.032; terminal gravity 1.005–1.008

Brewer's Specifics

1. Mash temperature: 150°F. at start. Mash time: 2 hours.
2. Add bittering hops 45 minutes before end of boil; add finishing hops 2 minutes before the end.
3. Pitching and fermentation temperature: 62–68°F.
4. Use 1 pint yeast starter or ½ cup slurry.
5. Isinglass finings may be added at bottling.
6. Store bottles 1 week at fermentation temperature, then 3 weeks at 50–60°F.

BROWN ALE (MILD)

Grains: 5.5 lbs. British pale ale malt; plus 8 oz. British crystal malt; plus 4 oz. chocolate malt

Sugar: 1 lb. dark brown sugar (add to boiler)

Bittering hops: 5 AAUs pellets or 6 AAUs whole hops — Fuggles, Goldings, or Northern Brewer

Finishing hops: none

Yeast: Wyeast Labs #1028 or #1098, or M.eV. Research #9

Priming sugar: ½ cup corn sugar

Gravities: original gravity 1.046; terminal gravity 1.007–1.010

Brewer's Specifics

1. Mash temperature: 150°F. at start. Mash time: 2 hours.
2. Add bittering hops 45 minutes before end of boil.
3. Pitching and fermentation temperature: 62–68°F.
4. Use 1 pint yeast starter or ½ cup slurry.
5. Isinglass finings may be added at bottling.
6. Store bottles 1 week at fermentation temperature, then 3 weeks at 50–60°F.

SCOTCH ALE

Grains: 7 lbs. British pale ale malt; plus 1 lb. British crystal malt; plus 4 oz. chocolate malt

Sugar: 1 lb. dark brown sugar (add to boiler)

Bittering hops: 7 AAUs pellets or 8 AAUs whole hops — Fuggles or Northern Brewer

Finishing hops: none

Yeast: Wyeast Labs #1098, or M.eV. Research #9

Priming sugar: ½ cup corn sugar

Gravities: original gravity 1.055; terminal gravity 1.010–1.014

Brewer's Specifics

1. Mash temperature: 150°F. at start. Mash time: 2 hours
2. Add bittering hops 45 minutes before end of boil.
3. Pitching and fermentation temperature: 62–68°F.
4. Use 1 pint yeast starter or ½ cup slurry.
5. Isinglass finings may be added at bottling.
6. Store bottles 1 week at fermentation temperature, then 3 weeks at 50–60°F.

OLD ALE

Grains: 8 lbs. British pale ale malt; plus 1 lb. 60°L. crystal malt; plus 8 oz. chocolate malt
Sugar: 24 oz. light molasses (add to boiler)
Bittering hops: 7 AAUs pellets or 8 AAUs whole hops — Fuggles or Northern Brewer
Finishing hops: none
Yeast: Wyeast Labs #1098 or #1084, or M.eV. Research #9 or #4
Priming sugar: ½ cup corn sugar or ⅓ cup firmly packed dark brown sugar
Gravities: original gravity 1.064; terminal gravity 1.012–1.016

Brewer's Specifics

1. Mash temperature: 150°F. at start. Mash time: 2 hours.
2. Add bittering hops 45 minutes before end of boil.
3. Pitching and fermentation temperature: 62–68°F.
4. Use 1 pint yeast starter or ½ cup slurry.
5. Isinglass finings may be added at bottling.
6. Store bottles 1 week at fermentation temperature, then 6 weeks at 50–60°F.

PORTER

Grains: 6.5 lbs. British pale ale malt; plus 6 oz. roasted barley

Bittering hops: 9 AAUs pellets or 11 AAUs whole hops — Northern Brewer or other high-alpha British hops

Finishing hops: none

Yeast: Wyeast Labs #1028 or #1084, or M.eV. Research #4

Priming sugar: ½ cup corn sugar

Gravities: original gravity 1.048; terminal gravity 1.010–1.014

Brewer's Specifics

1. Mash temperature: 150°F. at start. Mash time: 2 hours.
2. Add bittering hops 45 minutes before end of boil.
3. Pitching and fermentation temperature: 62–68°F.
4. Use 1 pint yeast starter or ½ cup slurry.
5. Isinglass finings may be added at bottling.
6. Store bottles 1 week at fermentation temperature, then 3 weeks at 50–60°F.

DRY STOUT

Grains: 6 lbs. British pale ale malt; plus 1 lb. flaked barley and 12 oz. roasted barley

Bittering hops: 10 AAUs pellets or 12 AAUs whole hops — Northern Brewer or other high-alpha British hops

Finishing hops: none

Yeast: Wyeast Labs #1028 or #1084, or M.eV. Research #4

Priming sugar: ½ cup corn sugar

Gravities: original gravity 1.048; terminal gravity 1.010–1.014

Brewer's Specifics

1. Mash temperature: 150°F. at start. Mash time: 2 hours.
2. Add bittering hops 45 minutes before end of boil.
3. Pitching and fermentation temperature: 62–68°F.
4. Use 1 pint yeast starter or ½ cup slurry.
5. Isinglass finings may be added at bottling.
6. Store bottles 1 week at fermentation temperature, then 3 weeks at 50–60°F.

SWEET STOUT

Grains: 6.5 lbs. British pale ale malt; plus 8 oz. British crystal malt; plus 6 oz. roasted barley

Bittering hops: 7 AAUs pellets or 8 AAUs whole hops — Northern Brewer or other high-alpha British hops

Finishing hops: none

Yeast: Wyeast Labs #1028 or #1084, or M.eV. Research #4

Priming sugar: ½ cup corn sugar or ⅓ cup firmly packed dark brown sugar

Gravities: original gravity 1.046; terminal gravity 1.010–1.014

Brewer's Specifics

1. Mash temperature: 152°F. at start. Mash time: 2 hours.
2. Add bittering hops 45 minutes before end of boil.
3. Pitching and fermentation temperature: 62–68°F.
4. Use 1 pint yeast starter or ½ cup slurry.
5. Isinglass finings may be added at bottling.
6. Store bottles 1 week at fermentation temperature, then 3 weeks at 50–60°F.

IMPERIAL STOUT

Grains: 10 lbs. British pale ale malt; plus 1 lb. British crystal malt; plus 8 oz. chocolate malt; plus 4 oz. roasted barley

Sugar: 1 lb. dark brown sugar (add to boiler)

Bittering hops: 10 AAUs pellets or 12 AAUs whole hops — Northern Brewer or other high-alpha British hops

Finishing hops: none

Yeast: Wyeast Labs #1056 or #1084, or M.eV. Research #72 or #4

Priming sugar: ½ cup corn sugar

Gravities: original gravity 1.083; terminal gravity 1.017–1.024

Brewer's Specifics

1. Mash temperature: 150°F. at start. Mash time: 2 hours.
2. Add bittering hops 45 minutes before end of boil.
3. Pitching and fermentation temperature: 62–68°F.
4. Use 1 pint yeast starter or ½ cup slurry. (Note: If fermentation hangs, the yeast may have been killed by the high alcohol content. Rack off, add 1 teaspoon yeast nutrient, and repitch with a packet of rehydrated champagne yeast.)
5. Isinglass finings may be added at bottling.
6. Store bottles 2 weeks at fermentation temperature, then 12 weeks at 50–60°F.

BARLEY WINE

Grains: 10 lbs. British pale ale malt; plus 12 oz. British crystal malt

Sugar: 1.5 lbs. light brown or raw sugar (add to boiler)

Bittering hops: 13 AAUs pellets or 15 AAUs whole hops — Fuggles, Goldings, or Northern Brewer

Finishing hops: none

Yeast: Wyeast Labs #1028 or #1056, or M.eV. Research #72

Priming sugar: ½ cup corn sugar

Gravities: original gravity 1.085; terminal gravity 1.017–1.023

Brewer's Specifics

1. Mash temperature: 150°F. at start. Mash time: 2 hours.
2. Add bittering hops 45 minutes before end of boil.
3. Pitching and fermentation temperature: 62–68°F.
4. Use 1 pint yeast starter or ½ cup slurry. (Note: If fermentation hangs, the yeast may have been killed by the high alcohol content. Rack off, add 1 teaspoon yeast nutrient, then repitch with a packet of rehydrated champagne yeast.)
5. Isinglass finings may be added at bottling.
6. Store bottles 2 weeks at fermentation temperature, then 12 weeks at 50–60°F.

ALTBIER

Grains: 6 lbs. pale 2-row malt; plus 1 lb. wheat malt (crush fine); plus 8 oz. 40°L. crystal malt; plus 1 oz. black malt
Bittering hops: 8 AAUs pellets or 10 AAUs whole hops — Hallertau, Tettnanger, Spalt, or Perle
Finishing hops: none
Yeast: Wyeast Labs #1007 or #1338, or M.eV. Research #3
Priming sugar: ¾ cup corn sugar
Gravities: original gravity 1.048; terminal gravity 1.010–1.015

Brewer's Specifics

1. Optional: Mash in at 122°F.; hold 30 minutes before raising to 152°F.
2. Mash temperature: 152°F. at start. Mash time: 2 hours.
3. Add two-thirds of bittering hops 45 minutes before end of boil; add remaining third 15 minutes before the end.
4. Pitching and fermentation temperature: 62–68°F.
5. Use 1 pint yeast starter or ½ cup slurry.
6. Isinglass finings may be added at bottling.
7. Store bottles 1 week at fermentation temperature, then 3 weeks at 40–50°F.

KOLSCH

Grains: 6 lbs. pale 2-row malt; plus 8 oz. wheat malt (crush fine); plus 4 oz.
Vienna malt

Bittering hops: 5 AAUs pellets or 6 AAUs whole hops — Hallertau,
Tettnanger, Spalt, or Perle

Finishing hops: none

Yeast: Wyeast Labs #1007 or #1338, or M.eV. Research #3

Priming sugar: ¾ cup corn sugar

Gravities: original gravity 1.044; terminal gravity 1.006–1.009.

Brewer's Specifics

1. Mash temperature: 150°F. at start. Mash time: 2 hours.

2. Add two-thirds of bittering hops 45 minutes before end of boil; add
remaining third 15 minutes before the end.

3. Pitching and fermentation temperature: 62–68°F.

4. Use 1 pint yeast starter or ½ cup slurry.

5. Isinglass finings may be added at bottling.

6. Store bottles 1 week at fermentation temperature, then 3 weeks at 40–
50°F.

WEISSBIER

Grains: 3.75 lbs. pale 2-row malt; plus 1.25 lbs. wheat malt (crush fine)

Bittering hops: 3.5 AAUs pellets or 4 AAUs whole hops — Hallertau,
Tettnanger, Spalt, or Perle

Finishing hops: none

Yeast: Wyeast Labs #1007 or #1338, or M.eV. Research #3

Priming sugar: 1 cup corn sugar

Gravities: original gravity 1.034; terminal gravity about 1.005

Brewer's Specifics

1. Optional: Mash in at 122°F.; hold 30 minutes before raising to 152°F.
2. Mash temperature: 152°F. at start. Mash time: 2 hours.
3. Add two-thirds of bittering hops 45 minutes before end of boil; add remaining third 15 minutes before the end.
4. Pitching and fermentation temperature: 62–68°F.
5. Use 1 pint yeast starter or ½ cup slurry.
6. Isinglass finings may be added at bottling. Lactic acid may also be added to taste if the tartness of authentic Berliner Weissbier is desired.
7. Store bottles 1 week at fermentation temperature, then 3 weeks at 50–60°F.

WEIZEN

Grains: 2.5 lbs. pale 2-row malt; plus 5 lbs. wheat malt (crush fine)
Bittering hops: 5 AAUs pellets or 6 AAUs whole hops — Hallertau, Tettnanger, Spalt, or Perle
Finishing hops: none
Yeast: Wyeast Labs #3056 or M.eV. Research #33
Priming sugar: 1 cup corn sugar
Gravities: original gravity 1.047; terminal gravity 1.008–1.012

Brewer's Specifics

1. Optional: Mash in at 122°F.; hold 30 minutes before raising to 150°F.
2. Mash temperature: 150°F. at start. Mash time: 2 hours.
3. Add two-thirds of bittering hops 45 minutes before end of boil; add remaining third 15 minutes before the end.
4. Pitching and fermentation temperature: 62–68°F.
5. Use 1 pint yeast starter or ½ cup slurry.
6. Isinglass finings may be added at bottling.
7. Store bottles 1 week at fermentation temperature, then 3 weeks at 40–50°F.

WIT

Grains: 4.5 lbs. pale 2-row malt; plus 2 lbs. wheat malt (crush fine) or flaked wheat

Bittering hops: 4 AAUs pellets or 5 AAUs whole hops — Hallertau, Fuggles, or Goldings

Finishing hops: none

Yeast: Wyeast Labs #1007 or #1338, or M.eV. Research #3

Special ingredient: 1 oz. coriander seed

Priming sugar: ¾ cup corn sugar

Gravities: original gravity 1.043; terminal gravity 1.006–1.008

Brewer's Specifics

1. Optional: Mash in at 122°F.; hold 30 minutes before raising to 152°F.
2. Mash temperature: 152°F. at start. Mash time: 2 hours.
3. Add two-thirds of bittering hops 45 minutes before end of boil; add remaining third 15 minutes before the end.
4. Pitching and fermentation temperature: 62–68°F.
5. Use 1 pint yeast starter or ½ cup slurry.
6. Crush coriander seeds and put into a 5-gallon carboy just before racking. Allow to sit 2 weeks before bottling.
7. Isinglass finings may be added at bottling.
8. Store bottles 1 week at fermentation temperature, then 3 weeks at 50–60°F.

TRAPPIST ALE

Grains: 9.5 lbs. pale 2-row malt; plus 1 lb. 40°L. crystal malt

Sugar: 1 lb. dark brown sugar (add to boiler)

Bittering hops: 9 AAUs pellets or 11 AAUs whole hops — Hallertau and Fuggles (50–50 blend)

Finishing hops: none

Yeast: Fresh culture from a Chimay ale bottle

Priming sugar: ½ cup corn sugar

Gravities: original gravity 1.076; terminal gravity 1.015–1.020

Brewer's Specifics

1. Mash temperature: 150°F. at start. Mash time: 2 hours.
2. Add two-thirds of bittering hops 45 minutes before end of boil; add remaining third 15 minutes before the end.
3. Pitching and fermentation temperature: 68–72°F.
4. Use 1 quart yeast starter (use two-step culture process as described on page 36).
5. Isinglass finings may be added at bottling.
6. Store bottles 2 weeks at fermentation temperature, then 12 weeks at 50–60°F.

FRUIT ALE

Grains: 4 lbs. pale 2-row malt; plus 2.5 lbs. wheat malt
Bittering hops: 1.5 AAUs pellets or 2 AAUs whole hops — any type
Finishing hops: none
Special ingredient: 10 lbs. cherries, raspberries, or peaches, washed and crushed (used in second fermentation)
Yeast: Wyeast Labs #1007 or #1338, or M.eV. Research #3
Priming sugar: 1¼ cups corn sugar
Gravities: original gravity 1.045; terminal gravity 1.008–1.012

Brewer's Specifics

1. Optional: Mash in at 122°F.; hold 30 minutes before raising to 155°F.
2. Mash temperature: 155°F. at start. Mash time: 1 hour.
3. Add all hops 45 minutes before end of boil.
4. Pitching and fermentation temperature: 62–68°F.
5. Use 1 pint yeast starter or ½ cup slurry.
6. After 7 days of fermentation, add the freshly prepared fruit to a second fermenter and rack the beer over it. Allow to ferment for 2 weeks before racking off into a 5-gallon carboy.
7. Isinglass finings may be added at bottling.
8. Store bottles 1 week at fermentation temperature, then 8 weeks at 50–60°F.

CREAM ALE

Grains: 5 lbs. pale 6-row malt; plus 4 oz. 10°L. crystal malt; plus 4 oz. dextrin (Cara-pils) malt; plus 1 lb. flaked maize (corn)

Bittering hops: 4 AAUs pellets or 5 AAUs whole hops — Hallertau, Tettnanger, Perle, or Cascade

Finishing hops: ½ oz. Tettnanger or Cascade

Yeast: Wyeast Labs #1056 or M.eV. Research #69

Priming sugar: ¾ cup corn sugar

Gravities: original gravity 1.043; terminal gravity 1.006–1.008

Brewer's Specifics

1. Optional: Mash in at 130°F.; hold 30 minutes before raising to 150°F.
2. Mash temperature: 150°F. at start. Mash time: 2 hours.
3. Add bittering hops 45 minutes before end of boil. Add whole finishing hops 5 minutes before end, pelletized finishing hops at end of boil.
4. Pitching and fermentation temperature: 62–68°F.
5. Use 1 pint yeast starter or ½ cup slurry.
6. Isinglass finings may be added at bottling.
7. Store bottles 1 week at fermentation temperature, then 3 weeks at 40–50°F.

CALIFORNIA COMMON BEER

Grains: 6 lbs. pale 2-row malt; plus 8 oz. Vienna malt; plus 8 oz. 40°L. crystal malt

Bittering hops: 10 AAUs pellets or 12 AAUs whole hops — Northern Brewer or Cascade

Finishing hops: 1.5 oz. Northern Brewer or Cascade

Yeast: Wyeast Labs #2007 or M.eV. Research #4

Priming sugar: ¾ cup corn sugar

Gravities: original gravity 1.045; terminal gravity 1.007–1.012.

Brewer's Specifics

1. Mash temperature: 154°F. at start. Mash time: 1½ hours.
2. Add two-thirds of bittering hops 45 minutes before end of boil; add remaining third 15 minutes before the end. Add whole finishing hops 5 minutes before the end, pelletized finishing hops at end of boil.
3. Pitching and fermentation temperature: 62–68°F.
4. Use 1 quart yeast starter or ⅔ cup slurry.
5. Store bottles 1 week at fermentation temperature, then 5 weeks at temperatures as cool as possible (32°F. minimum).

LIGHT-BODIED PILSNER

Grains: 5.5 lbs. pale 2-row malt; plus 1 lb. flaked maize (corn)
Bittering hops: 3.5 AAUs pellets or 4 AAUs whole hops — Hallertau, Tettnanger, or Cascade
Finishing hops: ½ oz. Tettnanger, Cascade, or Saaz
Yeast: Wyeast Labs #2007 or #2042, or M.eV. Research #4 or #55
Priming sugar: ¾ cup corn sugar
Gravities: original gravity 1.044; terminal gravity 1.006–1.010

Brewer's Specifics

1. Optional: Mash in at 130°F.; hold 30 minutes before raising to 150°F.
2. Mash temperature: 150°F. at start. Mash time: 2 hours.
3. Add two-thirds of bittering hops 45 minutes before end of boil; add remaining third 15 minutes before end. Add whole finishing hops 5 minutes before end, pelletized finishing hops at end of boil. (Note: For a European flavor, increase bittering hops to 5–7 AAUs and use Saaz finishing hops.)
4. Pitching and fermentation temperature: 50–55°F.
5. Use 1 quart yeast starter or ⅔ cup slurry.
6. Store bottles 10 days at fermentation temperature, then 4 weeks at temperatures as cool as possible (32°F. minimum).

CLASSIC ALL-MALT PILSNER

Grains: 7 lbs. 2-row pale malt; plus 8 oz. dextrin (Cara-pils) malt; plus 4 oz. 10°L. crystal malt

Bittering hops: 7–9 AAUs pellets or 9–11 AAUs whole hops — Hallertau, Tettnanger, or Cascade

Finishing hops: 1–1.5 oz. Saaz

Yeast: Wyeast Labs #2124, #2042, or #2308, or M.eV. Research #55 or #37

Priming sugar: ¾ cup corn sugar

Gravities: original gravity 1.050; terminal gravity 1.007–1.012

Brewer's Specifics

1. Optional: Mash in at 130°F.; hold 30 minutes before raising to 150°F.
2. Mash temperature: 150°F. at start. Mash time: 2 hours.
3. Add two-thirds of bittering hops 45 minutes before end of boil; add remaining third 15 minutes before end. Add whole finishing hops 5 minutes before the end, pelletized finishing hops at end of boil.
4. Pitching and fermentation temperature: 46–50°F.
5. Use 1 quart yeast starter or ⅔ cup slurry.
6. Store bottles 10 days at fermentation temperature, then 4 weeks at temperatures as cool as possible (32°F. minimum).

MUNICH HELLES

Grains: 6 lbs. pale 2-row malt; plus 8 oz. Vienna malt; plus 8 oz. dextrin (Cara-pils) malt

Bittering hops: 5 AAUs pellets or 6 AAUs whole hops — Hallertau, Tettnanger, Perle, or Mt. Hood

Finishing hops: ¼ oz. Tettnanger or Hallertau

Yeast: Wyeast Labs #2206 or #2308, or M.eV. Research #37

Priming sugar: ¾ cup corn sugar

Gravities: original gravity 1.045; terminal gravity 1.007–1.011

Brewer's Specifics

1. Optional: Mash in at 130°F.; hold 30 minutes before raising to 152°F.
2. Mash temperature: 152°F. at start. Mash time: 2 hours.
3. Add two-thirds of bittering hops 45 minutes before end of boil; add remaining third 15 minutes before end. Add whole finishing hops 5 minutes before the end, pelletized finishing hops at end of boil.
4. Pitching and fermentation temperature: 46–50°F.
5. Use 1 quart yeast starter or ⅔ cup slurry.
6. Store bottles 10 days at fermentation temperature, then 4 weeks at temperatures as cool as possible (32°F. minimum).

MUNICH DUNKEL

Grains: 5 lbs. pale 2-row malt; plus 2.5 lbs. Munich malt; plus 8 oz. 60°L. crystal malt; plus 1 oz. black malt

Bittering hops: 5 AAUs pellets or 6 AAUs whole hops — Hallertau, Tettnanger, Perle, or Mt. Hood

Finishing hops: none

Yeast: Wyeast Labs #2206 or #2308, or M.eV. Research #37

Priming sugar: ¾ cup corn sugar

Gravities: original gravity 1.049; terminal gravity 1.010–1.014

Brewer's Specifics

1. Mash temperature: 153°F. at start. Mash time: 1½ hours.
2. Add two-thirds of bittering hops 45 minutes before end of boil; add remaining third 15 minutes before end.
3. Pitching and fermentation temperature: 46–50°F.
4. Use 1 quart yeast starter or ⅔ cup slurry.
5. Store bottles 10 days at fermentation temperature, then 4 weeks at temperatures as cool as possible (32°F. minimum).

DORTMUNDER EXPORT

Grains: 7 lbs. pale 2-row malt; plus 1 lb. Vienna malt; plus 8 oz. dextrin (Cara-pils) malt

Bittering hops: 6 AAUs pellets or 7 AAUs whole hops — Hallertau, Tettnanger, Perle, or Mt. Hood

Finishing hops: ½ oz. Tettnanger or Hallertau

Yeast: Wyeast Labs #2206 or #2308, or M.eV. Research #37

Priming sugar: ¾ cup corn sugar

Gravities: original gravity 1.055; terminal gravity 1.011–1.015

Brewer's Specifics

1. Optional: Mash in at 130°F.; hold 30 minutes before raising to 152°F.
2. Mash temperature: 152°F. at start. Mash time: 2 hours.
3. Add two-thirds of bittering hops 45 minutes before end of boil; add remaining third 15 minutes before end. Add whole finishing hops 5 minutes before the end, pelletized finishing hops at end of boil.
4. Pitching and fermentation temperature: 46–50°F.
5. Use 1 quart yeast starter or ⅔ cup slurry.
6. Store bottles 10 days at fermentation temperature, then 5 weeks at temperatures as cool as possible (32°F. minimum).

OKTOBERFEST (MÄRZEN)

Grains: 5 lbs. pale 2-row malt; plus 3 lbs. Munich malt; plus 12 oz. dextrin (Cara-pils) malt; plus 4 oz. 40°L. crystal malt; plus ¼ oz. black malt

Bittering hops: 6 AAUs pellets or 7 AAUs whole hops — Hallertau, Tettnanger, Perle, or Mt. Hood

Finishing hops: none

Yeast: Wyeast Labs #2206 or #2308, or M.eV. Research #37

Priming sugar: ¾ cup corn sugar

Gravities: original gravity 1.054; terminal gravity 1.012–1.016

Brewer's Specifics

1. Mash temperature: 152°F. at start. Mash time: 2 hours.
2. Add two-thirds of bittering hops 45 minutes before end of boil; add remaining third 15 minutes before end.
3. Pitching and fermentation temperature: 46–50°F.
4. Use 1 quart yeast starter or two-thirds cup slurry.
5. Store bottles 10 days at fermentation temperature, then 6 weeks at temperatures as cool as possible (32°F. minimum).

HELLES BOCK

Grains: 8.5 lbs. pale 2-row malt; plus 1 lb. Vienna malt; plus 1 lb. dextrin (Cara-pils) malt; plus 4 oz. 20°L. crystal malt
Bittering hops: 7 AAUs pellets or 8 AAUs whole hops — Hallertau, Tettnanger, Perle, or Mt. Hood
Finishing hops: ¼ oz. Tettnanger or Hallertau
Yeast: Wyeast Labs #2206 or #2308, or M.eV. Research #37
Priming sugar: ¾ cup corn sugar
Gravities: original gravity 1.066; terminal gravity 1.014–1.018

Brewer's Specifics

1. Optional: Mash in at 130°F.; hold 30 minutes before raising to 152°F.
2. Mash temperature: 152°F. at start. Mash time: 2 hours.
3. Add two-thirds of bittering hops 45 minutes before end of boil; add remaining third 15 minutes before end. Add whole finishing hops 5 minutes before the end, pelletized finishing hops at end of boil.
4. Pitching and fermentation temperature: 46–50°F.
5. Use 1 quart yeast starter or two-thirds cup slurry.
6. Store bottles 14 days at fermentation temperature, then 8 weeks at temperatures as cool as possible (32°F. minimum).

DUNKEL BOCK

Grains: 6.25 lbs. pale 2-row malt; plus 2.25 lbs. Munich malt; plus 1 lb.
  dextrin (Cara-pils) malt; plus 1.5 lbs. 60°L. crystal malt
Bittering hops: 7 AAUs pellets or 8 AAUs whole hops — Hallertau,
  Tettnanger, Perle, or Mt. Hood
Finishing hops: none
Yeast: Wyeast Labs #2206 or #2308, or M.eV. Research #37
Priming sugar: ¾ cup corn sugar
Gravities: original gravity 1.065; terminal gravity 1.016–1.020

Brewer's Specifics

1. Mash temperature: 152°F. at start. Mash time: 2 hours.
2. Add two-thirds of bittering hops 45 minutes before end of boil; add
    remaining third 15 minutes before end.
3. Pitching and fermentation temperature: 46–50°F.
4. Use 1 quart yeast starter or ⅔ cup slurry.
5. Store bottles 14 days at fermentation temperature, then 8 weeks at
    temperatures as cool as possible (32°F. minimum).

DOPPELBOCK

Grains: 3.5 lbs. pale 2-row malt; plus 3 lbs. Munich malt; plus 1 lb. dextrin
  (Cara-pils) malt; plus 2 lbs. 60°L. crystal malt
Malt extract: 3.3 lbs. Northwestern pale syrup, unhopped (add to boiler)
Bittering hops: 7 AAUs pellets or 8 AAUs whole hops — Hallertau,
  Tettnanger, Perle, or Mt. Hood
Finishing hops: none
Yeast: Wyeast Labs #2206 or #2308, or M.eV. Research #37
Priming sugar: ¾ cup corn sugar
Gravities: original gravity 1.076; terminal gravity 1.020–1.024

Brewer's Specifics

1. Mash temperature: 152°F. at start. Mash time: 2 hours.
2. Add two-thirds of bittering hops 45 minutes before end of boil; add remaining third 15 minutes before end.
3. Pitching and fermentation temperature: 46–50°F.
4. Use 1 quart yeast starter or ⅔ cup slurry.
5. Store bottles 14 days at fermentation temperature, then 10 weeks at temperatures as cool as possible (32°F. minimum).

GOING SEMI-PRO

s explained in the Introduction, there are some steps in home brewing that do not fit into the progression of this book. These are purely optional and may be incorporated into your routine whenever you decide. They will not make better beer, but they all have certain advantages that make them worth considering.

USING DRAFT KEGS

Home brewing pioneer Byron Burch's Third Law states that, "The tendency of a home brewer to look favorably on the idea of kegging homebrew is directly proportional to the number of bottles washed during the course of his or her home-brewing career." That says it all. The only disadvantage of draft beer is the cost of the equipment. Prices for a basic kit, consisting of a CO_2 cylinder, pressure regulator, gauges, keg, lines, and fittings, range at the present time from $150 to $250. Additional kegs cost $25 to $45 each, used. Bottling versus kegging represents the classic tradeoff of money for convenience.

The prices cited above are for a system based on 5-gallon stainless steel kegs used for dispensing soda.

Figure 5–1. A basic draft beer setup, consisting of (left to right): CO_2 cylinder with regulator and gauges, gas line, soda keg, beer line, and serving tap.

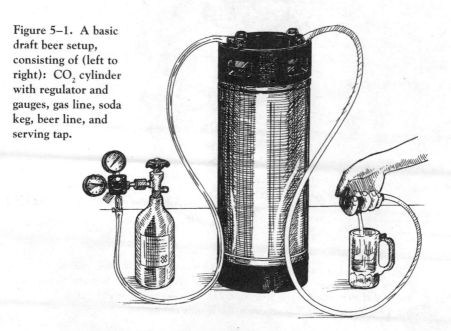

Other systems are available based on plastic vessels. Plastic is less expensive than stainless steel, but poses more problems with sanitation. From experience I will tell you that any system that uses tiny "seltzer bottle" CO_2 gas bulbs will cost you more in the long run than a soda-keg system.

There are two types of stainless steel soda kegs. The difference is in the type of fittings on the kegs: one uses pin-lock, the other ball-lock mechanisms to attach the gas and beer lines. Both work well — just make sure that all of the equipment you buy has fittings that correspond to the type of lock mechanism you are using.

Individual kegs will differ in the type of relief valve fitted to their lids. The best design is a valve that can be opened by hand to vent the pressure in the keg. Valves that cannot be vented are less desirable; the only way you can vent a keg with one of these valves is to press down on the gas fitting with a screwdriver. Doing this with a full keg will often deliver a faceful of beer.

There is one important change that must be made in brewing technique when you switch to draft beer. Bottled homebrew is put in its "package" relatively early, while the yeast is still fresh and capable of fermenting the priming sugar. With draft beer, on the other hand, you should

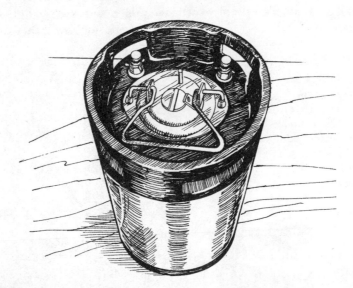

Figure 5–2. Top view of a soda keg. This is a pin-style keg: the gas fitting has two pins, the beer fitting three. On a ball-lock keg, the fittings are of different diameters, and connections must be made carefully. Marking the style of keg you're using avoids confusion.

age the beer in the carboy to allow as much yeast as possible to settle out. If you use isinglass finings to assist in clarifying your ales, you must add these finings to the carboy at racking, rather than at bottling time.

For lager beer, California common beer, and German ales, I recommend 3 to 5 weeks of cold storage at 32° to 34°F. in the carboy prior to kegging. For British ales of normal strength, 2 weeks at 40° to 45°F. is sufficient.

After your beer has been given cold storage as recommended, kegging is extremely simple. Sanitize and rinse the keg, lid, and fittings, along with your racking hose and tube. Rack the beer into the keg, collecting as much beer as possible, but being careful not to draw any sediment into the keg. Take the temperature of the beer using an accurate thermometer. Fit the lid, hook up your gas line, and apply 5 pounds of pressure. Turn off the gas and vent the keg, either by actuating the relief valve (if possible) or by disconnecting the gas line and pressing down on the fitting with a screwdriver. If you have to do this, try to tilt the keg so that the bottom of the gas inlet tube is not submerged in the beer. The idea is to vent the gas rather than spray yourself.

Repeat the pressurize-vent sequence three times. At this point, you have essentially replaced all the air above the beer with carbon dioxide gas. This is important to prevent oxidation.

After venting for the last time, you are ready to carbonate your beer. Carbonation is measured in volumes of CO_2. A liter of beer containing three liters of CO_2 (at standard temperature and pressure) is said to contain 3 volumes of CO_2. This is high carbonation for beer. I recommend 1.8 to 2.2 volumes for British ales, 2.5 volumes for lagers and German ales, and 3.0 volumes for wheat beers and fruit ales. American beers are usually carbonated at 2.6 to 2.8 volumes.

To get the right degree of carbonation, refer to the chart on pages 132-133. Find the temperature of the beer, then look across until you reach the carbonation level desired. Look up to the top of that column to find the required pressure, and set your regulator accordingly.

The easiest way to carbonate is to set the keg horizontally on a padded fulcrum and rock it back and forth until you no longer hear gas flowing through the keg fitting. This indicates that the pressure has equalized and no more CO_2 is being dissolved in the beer. In doing this, you should observe two cautions: first, rotate the keg so that the gas fitting is as high as possible. As the gas dissolves and the pressures in the line and keg equalize, beer can flow out of the gas fitting into the line. You want to prevent this if possible. Second, always position the gas cylinder well above the keg. If beer should get into the gas line, you do not want it to reach the regulator!

If it proves impossible to carbonate your beer without getting beer in the gas line, no real harm has been done: you just have to disassemble the line and sanitize the hose and lock mechanism. However, to prevent a repeat performance, you may want to use a more elaborate routine. That is, apply the correct pressure, then disconnect the gas line and rock for 30 seconds. Reconnect the gas line, restore the pressure, then remove it once again before rocking. You will have to repeat this sequence 20 times or more. Discontinue when no more gas flows into the keg.

After carbonating your beer, shut off the gas and disconnect the line. Store the keg in a refrigerator or other cool place at serving temperature (55°F. for British ales, 45°F. for German ales and lagers) for at least 3 days before tapping. It is best to store the keg on its side: that way, any sediment will stick to the wall of the keg, rather than the bottom, and you will be able to draw off clear beer when you set the keg upright for tapping.

If you have time, you can carbonate your draft beer without agitation, simply by storing the keg for 3 weeks or so with the gas line hooked up to it. In this case, set the pressure according to the temperature of the storage cellar or refrigerator, rather than the temperature of the beer.

Regardless of the pressure you applied for carbonation, and regardless of the level of carbonation in your beer, you should dispense it under 10 to 14 pounds of pressure. Sometimes people encounter foam-ing troubles and try to alleviate them by lowering the dispense pressure. This actually increases foaming. The best way to avoid foaming with draft beer is the same as with bottled beer: keep it cool and don't shake it up. Shaken beer is going to foam no matter what you do.

Another point about tapping: changes in temperature, as well as agitation, can result in high pressure in the keg. If this happens, the dispense pressure in the line may be lower than the keg pressure, and if your keg is full, beer could back up into the gas line, just as it can during carbonation. To prevent this, always vent the keg before attaching your gas line.

FILTRATION AND COUNTERPRESSURE BOTTLING

These techniques require a draft beer system, as described in the previous section, and they require additional equipment as well. They are not for the faint of heart or faint of pocketbook. On the other hand, they will give you sparkling, sediment-free beer fully comparable to commercial brews in appearance, as well as taste. Still, no matter how seriously you take home brewing, you should understand the hazards of filtration before you take the plunge.

The first is that filtration, if overdone, can remove body and even color from beer. The second concern is that filtered beers are more

We'd love your thoughts...

Your reactions, criticisms, things you did or didn't like about this Storey Book. Please use space below (or write a letter if you'd prefer — even send photos!) telling how you've made use of the information . . . how you've put it to work . . . the more details the better! Thanks in advance for your help in building our library of good Storey Books.

Pamela B. Art

Publisher

Book Title: _____

Purchased From: _____

Comments: _____

_____

_____

_____

_____

_____

_____

Your Name: _____

Address: _____

☐ Please check here if you'd like our latest Storey's Books for Country Living Catalog.

☐ You have my permission to quote from my comments, and use these quotations in ads, brochures, mail, and other promotions used to market your books.

Signed _____ Date _____

APRIL 1994

From: _____

_____

_____

_____

BUSINESS REPLY MAIL

FIRST CLASS MAIL   PERMIT NO. 2   POWNAL, VT

POSTAGE WILL BE PAID BY ADDRESSEE

STOREY'S BOOKS FOR COUNTRY LIVING
STOREY COMMUNICATIONS, INC.
105 SCHOOLHOUSE ROAD
POWNAL VT 05261-9988

NO POSTAGE
NECESSARY
IF MAILED
IN THE
UNITED STATES

susceptible to infection and oxidation than unfiltered ones, so good sanitation and careful technique are very important. However, to keep things in perspective, you have to remember that almost all commercial breweries filter their beer. If they can do it successfully, then so can you.

Filtration

Filtration requires, in addition to the basic draft beer equipment kit, a filter assembly of some sort and at least one extra soda keg. The basic procedure is to push the beer out of one keg, through the filter, and into the second keg, using carbon dioxide pressure.

The first choice you have to make is the filter apparatus itself. The only ready-to-use filter unit designed for home brewers is the Marcon unit (Marcon Filters, 40 Beverly Hills Drive, Downsview, Ontario, Canada M31 1A1). Another good choice is a 10-inch cartridge (the type sold for home water filtration) combined with a 3- or 5-micron absolute-rated pleated filter. This arrangement is less expensive, but requires some adaptation for filtering homebrew. Details are beyond the scope of this book, but there is an excellent article by Rodney Morris that describes the modi-

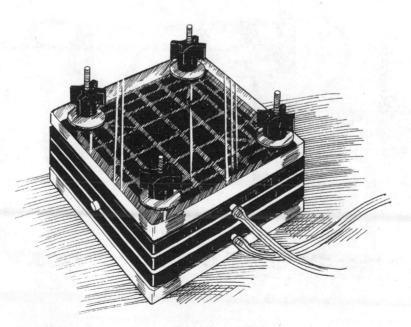

Figure 5–3. The Marcon filter, designed for use by home brewers.

fications necessary and lists sources (see Bibliography).

The first step in filtering beer is to rack it into a sanitized keg. You should not carbonate it, however — just purge the air from the headspace. Beer is easier to filter when it is flat. Chill it overnight to a temperature as close to freezing (32°F.) as possible, in order to form chill haze. Remember that, if you filter the beer warm, chill haze will not be removed.

The next step is to prepare the filter. First, assemble the filter and connect it to an empty keg. Fill the keg with dilute bleach solution, close the lid, then attach the gas fitting and push the chlorine solution through the filter and down the drain. Always position a plate-and-frame filter (such as the Marcon) over a pan or sink during use, since this type of filter "weeps" a little. Once the chlorine has been pushed through, disconnect the lines from the keg, rinse it several times, and refill with clean, sterile water. Seal the keg, reattach the hoses, and push the water through the filter. This serves two purposes: it flushes the chlorine out of the filter, and, at the same time, it fills the keg with CO_2.

When the filter has been flushed, disconnect the hoses from the empty keg. Get out your cold keg of beer

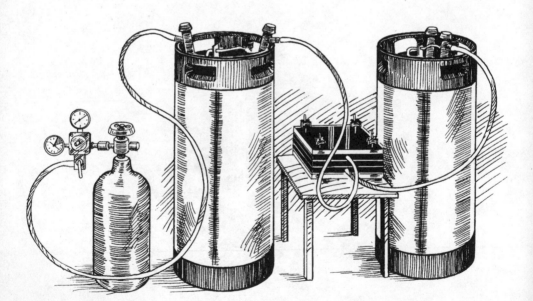

Figure 5–4. A basic filtration setup. Gas pressure is applied to the keg of unfiltered beer (left), and the beer is pushed through the filter into the empty keg (right).

and hook up the gas cylinder to the gas fitting and the filter line to the beer fitting. Turn on the gas and apply just enough pressure to push beer through the filter. Taste the beer as it flows out of the filter: the first pint or two will be watery. As soon as it regains its normal color and flavor, shut off the gas, vent the pressure on the beer keg, and connect the filter to the beer fitting of the empty keg. Vent the empty keg, then turn on the gas and apply about 10 to 15 pounds of pressure. You will have to vent the empty keg periodically, or fix its relief valve in the open position, while the beer is being filtered into it.

When all the beer has been filtered, shut off the gas, disconnect all hoses, and carbonate the filtered beer in the normal way. Clean and sanitize everything. The best way to clean a pleated filter is by washing it in hot water. The filter pads of the Marcon unit are single-use items.

Counterpressure Bottling

Counterpressure bottling is a natural extension of a keg system. It is a way to get a few bottles of sparkling clear beer for easy transport to parties, competitions, or other events when you don't want to lug a keg around. The basic item needed is a counterpressure filling device, which can be built fairly easily (plans published in the Spring 1990 issue of *zymurgy* — see Bibliography) or bought ready-made (manufactured by Foxx Equipment Co., 421 Southwest Blvd., Kansas City, Missouri 64108).

The first thing to remember about counterpressure filling is that it takes a little experience to get it right. No amount of description will prevent a few mishaps as you master the procedure. With that little warning in mind, let's look at how it works.

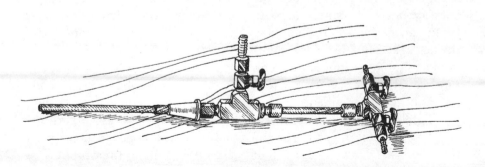

Figure 5–5. A counterpressure bottle filler.

A counterpressure filler is basically two tubes, one inside the other, and both surrounded by a stopper or gasket to seal the mouth of the bottle when the tubes are inserted. There are two ways it can be used, depending on how it is set up and what your layout is. In both methods, counterpressure is applied to the bottle during filling in order to prevent loss of carbonation. This is its great advantage over ordinary filling devices.

In the first method, gas pressure on the beer in the keg and inside the bottle are equal, and beer flows into the bottle by force of gravity. In the second method, the pressures are at first equal, but then the pressure in the bottle is lowered just enough to allow the beer to flow. The advantage of this second method is that the keg does not have to be elevated above the level of the bottles. The disadvantage is that the operation is more complicated and delicate.

The preliminary steps are the same for both methods: first, chill the beer down to 32°F. Unless the beer is very cold, foaming is liable to be unmanageable. If possible, wrap the keg in an insulated blanket during bottling, to minimize temperature rise during the operation. Clean and sanitize all equipment.

To fill by gravity flow (first method), first close all the valves on the filler device. Then hook up your lines as shown in Figure 5–6, with the gas connected to the keg and to the lower fitting of the filler (the one connected to the outer tube).

Connect the beer line to one of the upper fittings (the ones connected to the inner tube). Set the keg a couple of feet above the work surface. Open the valve on the gas cylinder and set the regulator to 15 pounds of pressure. Place the filler in the first bottle and open the beer line valve for a few seconds to allow beer to flow into the line. Then shut off the beer line and open the gas line valve. Let the pressure build up for a few seconds, then open the beer valve and let the beer flow into the bottle. When the bottle is filled to half an inch below the rim, shut off the beer. Then shut off the gas, remove the filler, and place it in the next bottle. Immediately cap the first bottle. Warning: as soon as you remove the filler, the bottle will start to foam over. Stay calm, but make haste!

To fill successive bottles, repeat the sequence above: open the gas line, open the beer line, fill the bottle, close the beer line, close the gas line, remove the filler, cap the bottle. It sounds a little complicated, but, after you do it a few times, you'll find yourself getting the hang of the routine.

The second method of using the counterpressure filler requires a different arrangement of the lines. The beer line and gas line are both attached to the upper fitting, which leads to the small inner tube. The outer tube is used to reduce pressure in the bottle so that beer can flow (see Figure 5–7, page 124).

To use this method, first turn off

all the valves on the filler, and connect the lines to the filler and keg as shown. Next, open the valve on the gas cylinder and set the regulator to 15 pounds of pressure. Insert the filler into the first bottle. Open the gas valve, then the lower (bleed) valve slightly, to purge the bottle of air. After 5 seconds, close the bleed valve and wait a few seconds for the bottle to pressurize. Close the gas valve. Then open the beer valve, and open the bleed valve slightly — just enough to allow the beer to flow smoothly into the bottle. It takes some experimenting to find the optimum setting that will give minimum foaming during the fill. Allow excess foam to escape through the bleed valve.

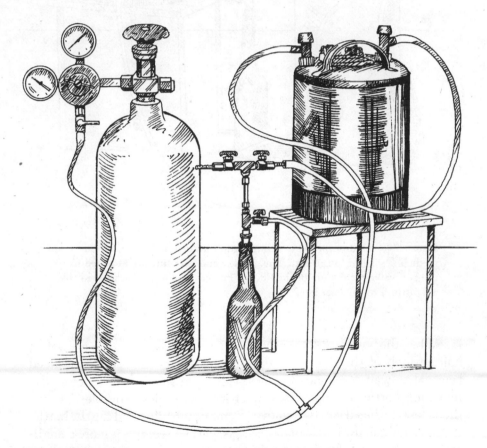

Figure 5–6. Counterpressure filling setup for bottling by the gravity-flow method. The gas line is attached to the lower valve of the filler, the beer line to one of the two upper valves. The T connector allows you to apply gas pressure to both the beer keg and the filler.

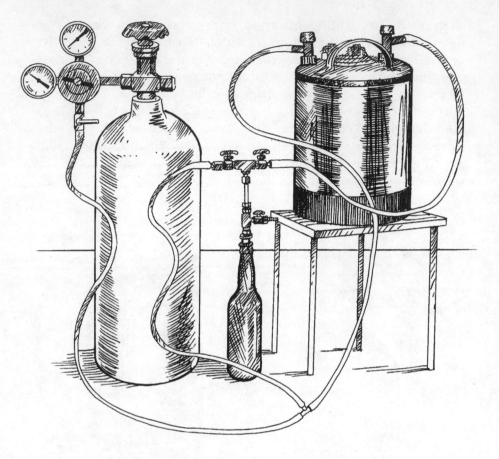

Figure 5–7. Counterpressure filling setup for bottling by the second method described in the text. The gas line and beer line are attached to the two valves at the top of the filler.   The gas line is also connected (by a T fitting) to the beer keg.

When the bottle is full to within half an inch of the rim, close the beer valve, wait 5 seconds for the remaining bottle pressure to escape, then close the bleed valve. Remove the filler and cap the bottle immediately.   Proceed to the next bottle and repeat the same sequence of steps: open the gas valve, open the bleed valve for 5 seconds, close the bleed valve, pressurize the bottle for a few seconds, close the gas valve, open the beer valve, open the bleed valve and fill the bottle, close the beer valve, close the bleed valve, remove the filler, and cap the bottle. As you can see, this is more complicated than the first (gravity-flow) method, but it does work well.

With either method of counterpressure filling, but especially with the second, a small loss of carbonation may occur during bottling. For this reason, you may wish to slightly overcarbonate your beer in the keg prior to bottling.

LARGE-BATCH BREWING

If you have gotten serious enough about brewing to be interested in filtration and other advanced techniques, you have also discovered that there is no such thing as an adequate supply of homebrew. Unless your life differs from most, there simply is not enough time to make it. This is where large-batch brewing comes in. It takes just as long to make 5 gallons at a time as 10, so the obvious way to increase your brewing efficiency is to double your batch size.

The easiest and cheapest way to get a couple of 14-gallon kettles — suitable for mashing and boiling 10-gallon batches — is to cut one end off a couple of half-barrel Sankey-type draft beer kegs. (This is the

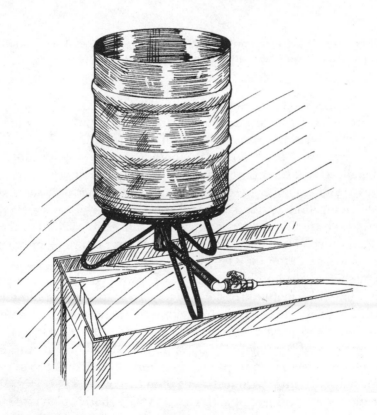

Figure 5–8. A 14-gallon stainless steel kettle, made from a commercial half-barrel beer keg, can be used for large-batch brewing. It is shown sitting on a King Kooker burner.

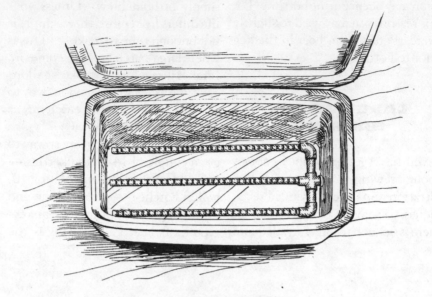

Figure 5–9. A lauter tun for large-batch brewing can be made from a 48-quart picnic cooler fitted with a manifold of slotted copper pipe.

style of keg that has only one valve fitting in one end.) You can scrounge these up yourself, if you know someone who can use a torch and can weld handles on the sides, or you can buy them from a number of suppliers. Fifteen-gallon stainless steel kettles, used by restaurants, are also excellent, though more expensive.

The best lauter tun for a large-scale masher is a 48-quart picnic cooler fitted with a manifold of slotted copper pipe. Complete plans for such a lauter tun have been published in *Beer and Brewing*, vol. 10 (see Bibliography). The only problem you may encounter with such a lauter tun is too rapid sparging. In order to get all the sugar out of the spent grains, adjust the flow so that sparging takes an hour to complete.

When you go to 10-gallon batches, you have just about outgrown your kitchen stove. I recommend moving your brewhouse outdoors or into the basement and using a propane-fired burner unit such as the King Kooker (formerly called the Cajun Heater). Such burners are available at most homebrew supply shops.

For wort cooling, you can make a larger version of your old reliable immersion cooler. Use 100 feet of ¼-inch i.d. tubing. After cooling, split your 10-gallon batch into two 5-gallon lots and ferment in two 7-gallon carboys.

An alternative plan is to build a tower brewhouse similar to the ones favored in old-style breweries. This system requires three large kettles, each fitted with a tap near the bottom (see Figure 5–10). The middle kettle is a combination mash/lauter tun. The tap of this kettle is attached to a length of flexible copper tubing, which has been slotted and coiled to fit inside the kettle.

A tower brewhouse is more expensive to build, partly because of the additional complexity of the kettles, and also because each of the kettles must have its own burner. The advantage is that you do not have to do any lifting to move liquid from one vessel to another. The only lugging you have to do is hauling the carboys from the brewhouse to the fermenting area, and even that can be avoided if you put the brewhouse in your basement and build a small wheeled cart to roll the vessels around.

A final word of caution: if you go in for large-scale brewing, be sure to provide adequate ventilation, not only to get rid of the steam, but also

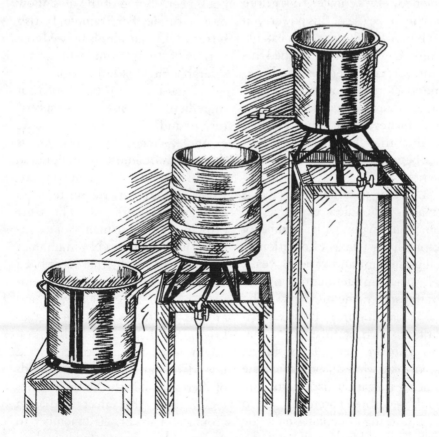

Figure 5–10. A tower brewhouse setup for large-scale brewing.

the exhaust gases from the burners. In a tight, unvented basement, carbon monoxide levels can quickly build up to dangerous levels when operating a large heating unit.

FORMULATING YOUR OWN RECIPES

One of the best aspects of home brewing is that you are free to make beer that tastes the way you think it should. You don't have to settle for somebody else's choices. But before you can make use of this power, you first have to be able to get repeatable results. Once you have reached this point, you can experiment and fine-tune your formulations with the confidence that it is really the ingredients, rather than some random variable, that has made the difference between one batch of beer and the next.

Learning to formulate recipes is a matter of endless experimentation. You can play with a number of factors: hops (times of addition as well as amount and variety), yeast, malt, mash and fermentation temperatures, to name just a few. The key to learning from these experiments, though, is this: *only change one variable at a time*. For instance, suppose you want to learn about the properties of various dark malts. You could brew three batches of brown ale, one using chocolate malt, the second using black malt, and the third using roasted barley. This will yield some enlightening and dra-

matic results, but you have to keep all the other ingredients the same, as well as all the procedures. Even a seemingly insignificant change — such as switching to a different brand of pale malt extract — will invalidate your results.

In making up your recipes, I suggest that you not stray too far from the specifications laid down in this book, especially when you are brewing lager beers. For example, you cannot arbitrarily decide to make a 1.060 Munich helles or a 1.040 bock beer. Some of the ales allow more latitude. For example, British bitter (draft pale ale) is brewed in a variety of strengths and with a considerable range of bitterness.

If you know a little about your ingredients, it is easy to make substitutions and observe the effects. One example, already familiar to you, is that you must adjust the hopping so that bitterness will remain constant when you are experimenting with different hop varieties. The same principle applies to malt. For example, Vienna malt and Munich malt are both pale malts that have been kilned at relatively high temperatures to develop color, flavor, and aroma. The first is rated at 4 degrees Lovibond, the second at 10. You might want to substitute, say, .2 pounds of Munich malt for .5 pounds of Vienna malt in the Munich Helles recipe, to see what effect that has on aroma and flavor. (Remember to increase the amount of pale malt so as to get the same original gravity.)

The flavor variations among

TABLE OF COMMON BREWING INGREDIENTS

Malt Type	Yield (SG pts./lb./gal.)	Color (degrees Lovibond)
Pale 2-row (domestic)	35	1.7
Pale 6-row (domestic)	33	1.7
British pale ale	36	3
British mild ale	33	5
Vienna malt (domestic)	32	4
Munich malt (domestic)	28	10
Cara-pils malt (domestic)	30	1.7
Crystal malt (domestic)	24	10–120
British crystal malt	26	55
Chocolate malt	24	350
Black malt (domestic)	24	540
Roasted barley	24	500
Flaked maize (corn)	40	0
Flaked barley	30	0
Brown sugar	45	15
Malt extract (syrup)	35	varies*
Malt extract (dry)	45	varies*

*Pale malt extracts can be anywhere between 3 and 10 degrees Lovibond.

yeast strains, hop varieties, and malt types are not easy to quantify, but malt does have some specifications, which are given in the table on page 129. These values should make it easier to formulate equivalent recipes using different types of malt.

The table can be used to derive approximate substitutions both in terms of yield (the amount of sugar, and hence the specific gravity of the wort) and color. I warn you, though, that color is complicated, and many substitutions will give surprising results. The numbers are just a guide to help you get started.

Color is figured using a very simple concept called the *color unit*. One color unit (CU) represents 1 pound of malt with a color rating of 1 degree Lovibond, or any equivalent, such as .1 pound of 10°L. malt. To calculate color, you must first multiply the weight (in pounds) of each malt in your recipe by the malt's color rating. Then add up the figures and divide by the number of gallons in the recipe. The following example is a recipe for 5 gallons of pale ale:

6 lbs. pale ale malt (3°L.)
   = 18 CUs (6 x 3)
.5 lb. British crystal malt (55°L.)
   = 27.5 CUs (55 x .5)

Total
   = 45.5 CUs
CUs per gallon
   = 9.1 (45.5 ÷ 5)

As a very rough guide, beers with 2 CUs per gallon will be yellow; 5 CUs per gallon, golden; 8 CUs per gallon, light amber; 12 CUs per gallon, deep amber; 16 CUs per gallon, light brown or copper, depending on the dark malt used. Crystal malt gives a reddish hue; black and chocolate malt are brown. Beers of 20 to 25 CUs per gallon are brown; beers over 30 are dark brown or black.

The original gravity of a brew can be calculated in a similar fashion. The *yield* of any grain is the number of specific gravity (SG) points that 1 pound will raise 1 gallon of water. For example, 1 pound of pale ale malt should raise the (SG) of a gallon of water from 1.000 to 1.036 (yield = 36 points). To predict the original gravity of a recipe, multiply the yield of each grain by the number of pounds, and divide by the batch size in gallons. Using the same example:

6 lbs. British pale malt
   = 216 SG points (36 x 6)
.5 lb. British crystal malt
   = 13 SG points (26 x .5)

Total
   = 229 SG points
Original gravity of wort
   = 46 or 1.046 (229 ÷ 5)

You may find, with experience, that the yield figures in the table do not match your results. You can adjust them downward if necessary.

However, the numbers given are what I actually get in my home brewery, and, if your numbers are lower, consider the following items, which may be responsible for a low yield of sugar from your malt:

1. Badly crushed malt. If some grains remain intact, they will not be converted during the mash.

2. Improper mash conditions — that is, pH or temperature. For optimum yield, mash pH should be between 5.0 and 5.8 and the starting temperature should be between 150° and 158° F.

3. Too short a mash time. Mash for 1 hour at the high end of the temperature range, 1½ to 2 hours at the low end.

4. Low sparge water temperature. Maintain sparge water between 168° and 155°F. during sparging.

5. Insufficient sparge water. Use at least 4 gallons for a 5-gallon batch.

6. Too short a sparge time. Regulate the outflow from the lauter tun so that the sparge proper — the rinsing of the grain with water — takes at least 45 minutes.

CARBONATION CHART

Pounds per Square Inch

Temp (°F)	1	2	3	4	5	6	7	8	9	10	11	12	13	14	15
30	1.82	1.92	2.03	2.14	2.23	2.36	2.48	2.60	2.70	2.82	2.93	3.02			
31	1.78	1.88	2.00	2.10	2.20	2.31	2.42	2.54	2.65	2.76	2.86	2.96			
32	1.75	1.85	1.95	2.05	2.16	2.27	2.38	2.48	2.59	2.70	2.80	2.90	3.01		
33		1.81	1.91	2.01	2.12	2.23	2.33	2.43	2.53	2.63	2.74	2.84	2.96		
34		1.78	1.86	1.97	2.07	2.18	2.28	2.38	2.48	2.58	2.68	2.79	2.89	3.00	
35			1.83	1.93	2.03	2.14	2.24	2.34	2.43	2.52	2.62	2.73	2.83	2.93	3.02
36			1.79	1.88	1.99	2.09	2.20	2.29	2.39	2.47	2.57	2.67	2.77	2.86	2.96
37				1.84	1.94	2.04	2.15	2.24	2.34	2.42	2.52	2.62	2.72	2.80	2.90
38				1.80	1.90	2.00	2.10	2.20	2.29	2.38	2.47	2.57	2.67	2.75	2.85
39					1.86	1.96	2.05	2.15	2.25	2.34	2.43	2.52	2.61	2.70	2.80
40					1.82	1.92	2.01	2.10	2.20	2.30	2.39	2.47	2.56	2.65	2.75
41						1.87	1.97	2.06	2.16	2.25	2.35	2.43	2.52	2.60	2.70
42						1.83	1.93	2.02	2.12	2.21	2.30	2.39	2.47	2.56	2.65
43						1.80	1.90	1.99	2.08	2.17	2.25	2.34	2.43	2.52	2.60
44							1.86	1.95	2.04	2.13	2.21	2.30	2.39	2.47	2.56
45							1.82	1.91	2.00	2.08	2.17	2.26	2.34	2.42	2.51
46								1.88	1.96	2.04	2.13	2.22	2.30	2.38	2.47
47								1.84	1.92	2.00	2.09	2.18	2.25	2.34	2.42
48								1.80	1.88	1.96	2.05	2.14	2.21	2.30	2.38
49									1.85	1.93	2.01	2.10	2.18	2.25	2.34
50									1.82	1.90	1.98	2.06	2.14	2.21	2.30
51										1.87	1.95	2.02	2.10	2.18	2.25
52										1.84	1.91	1.99	2.06	2.14	2.22
53										1.80	1.88	1.96	2.03	2.10	2.18
54											1.85	1.93	2.00	2.07	2.15
55											1.82	1.89	1.97	2.04	2.11
56												1.86	1.93	2.00	2.07
57												1.83	1.90	1.97	2.04
58												1.80	1.86	1.94	2.00
59													1.83	1.90	1.97
60													1.80	1.87	1.94

Temperature of Beer (degrees F.)

To Use This Chart: First find the temperature of your beer in the outside columns. Look across until you reach the carbonation level desired. Then look up to the top of that column to find the required pressure, and set your regulator accordingly.

This chart was adapted from one provided courtesy of Byron Burch, Great Fermentations of Santa Rosa, 840 Piner Road, #14, Santa Rosa, CA 95403. Used by permission.

CARBONATION CHART

Pounds per Square Inch

16	17	18	19	20	21	22	23	24	25	26	27	28	29	30	Temperature of Beer (degrees F.)
															30
															31
															32
															33
															34
															35
															36
3.00															37
2.94															38
2.89	2.98														39
2.84	2.93	3.01													40
2.79	2.87	2.96													41
2.74	2.82	2.91	3.00												42
2.69	2.78	2.86	2.95												43
2.64	2.73	2.81	2.90	2.99											44
2.60	2.68	2.77	2.85	2.94	3.02										45
2.55	2.63	2.72	2.80	2.89	2.98										46
2.50	2.59	2.67	2.75	2.84	2.93	3.02									47
2.46	2.55	2.62	2.70	2.79	2.87	2.96									48
2.42	2.50	2.58	2.66	2.75	2.83	2.91	2.99								49
2.38	2.45	2.54	2.62	2.70	2.78	2.86	2.94	3.02							50
2.34	2.41	2.49	2.57	2.65	2.73	2.81	2.89	2.97							51
2.30	2.37	2.45	2.54	2.61	2.69	2.76	2.84	2.93	3.00						52
2.26	2.33	2.41	2.48	2.57	2.64	2.72	2.80	2.88	2.95	3.03					53
2.22	2.29	2.37	2.44	2.52	2.60	2.67	2.75	2.83	2.90	2.98					54
2.19	2.25	2.33	2.40	2.47	2.55	2.63	2.70	2.78	2.85	2.93	3.01				55
2.15	2.21	2.29	2.36	2.43	2.50	2.58	2.65	2.73	2.80	2.88	2.96				56
2.11	2.18	2.25	2.33	2.40	2.47	2.54	2.61	2.69	2.76	2.84	2.91	2.99			57
2.07	2.14	2.21	2.29	2.36	2.43	2.50	2.57	2.64	2.72	2.80	2.86	2.94	3.01		58
2.04	2.11	2.18	2.25	2.32	2.39	2.46	2.53	2.60	2.67	2.75	2.81	2.89	2.96	3.03	59
2.01	2.08	2.14	2.21	2.28	2.35	2.42	2.49	2.56	2.63	2.70	2.77	2.84	2.91	2.98	60

The numbers in the grid express the volumes of carbon dioxide (CO_2); a liter of beer containing three liters of CO_2 (at standard temperature and pressure) is said to contain 3 volumes of CO_2. Suggested carbonation rates for various styles of beer can be found on page 117.

GLOSSARY

AAU. Alpha Acid Unit. A measure of alpha acid added to the wort at boiling. One ounce of 1 percent alpha hops contains one AAU.

Adjunct. Any unmalted grain used as a source of sugar in brewing.

Aerate. To dissolve air in a liquid.

Airlock. A device that allows carbon dioxide to escape from a fermenter, while preventing air from entering.

Ale. Beer made with ale yeast (*Saccharomyces cerevesiae*), often with a fruity aroma caused by fermenting at relatively warm temperatures.

Alpha acid. A sticky, bitter resin found in hops, which imparts bitterness to the finished beer. Also called *humulone*.

Bacteria. Primitive microorganisms, smaller than yeast. Certain types of bacteria can infect wort and beer and lead to off-flavors.

Bactericide. A substance that can kill bacteria. Chlorine is the best known in home brewing.

Bacteriostat. A substance that inhibits the growth of bacteria, but does not kill them. Sodium met-

abisulfite (Campden tablets) is an example.

Bittering hops. Hops added to the wort early in the boil to bitter it.

Body. *See* Mouthfeel.

Bottle-conditioned. Carbonated by a second fermentation that takes place in the bottle.

Bottom-fermenting. Describes yeast that flocculates late in the fermentation and sinks to the bottom of the fermenter.

Break. Visible particles of protein and other matter that form in wort during boiling and cooling. *See also* Trub.

Brewing. The process of making wort, boiling it with hops, and fermenting it into beer.

Carbonation. The process of dissolving carbon dioxide gas in a liquid, such as beer.

Carboy. A large glass bottle, 7 or 5 gallons in capacity, used as a fermenter in home brewing.

Chill haze. Tiny particles that form in beer when it is chilled and make it cloudy.

Clarifier. A substance used to remove or prevent chill haze.

Conversion. The process in which natural malt enzymes change grain starch into sugar during the mash.

Dextrins. Complex carbohydrates that contribute to the mouthfeel of beer.

Diacetyl. A compound that gives beer a taste reminiscent of butter or butterscotch.

Dry. Opposite of sweet. In a dry beer, bitterness predominates over sweetness.

F. Abbreviation for *Fahrenheit*, the scale used to measure temperature in the United States.

Fermentation. The metabolism of sugar into carbon dioxide and alcohol, performed by yeast and some bacteria.

Fermenter. A vessel used to contain wort during fermentation.

Finings. Any substance used to help yeast flocculate and settle out after fermentation.

Finishing hops. Hops added to the wort late in the boil, to impart a hoppy aroma rather than bitterness.

Flakes. Specially processed adjunct grains which can be added to the mash kettle without cooking.

Flocculation. The process in which yeast cells clump together to form large, visible particles.

High-alpha hops. Hop varieties bred primarily for high alpha acid content (that is, bittering power). Most useful as bittering hops.

Hop rate. The ratio of hops to wort (for example, 8 AAUs per 5 gallons).

Hops. The cones (flowers) of the female *Humulus lupulus* plant. They may be dried whole (whole hops) or processed into pellets.

Hydrometer. An instrument which measures the specific gravity of a liquid. *See also* Specific Gravity.

Infection. The growth of any microorganism in wort or beer, except for the brewer's yeast that was deliberately added. Most infections harm the flavor of the finished product.

Isinglass. A fining agent, made from the swim bladder of the stur-

geon. *See also* Finings.

Kraeusen. The large, irregular head of foam that forms on the surface of the wort as fermentation comes to a peak. The word means "crown" in German.

L. Abbreviation for *Lovibond* (see below).

Lactic acid. A tart acid, produced by yeast and, in much larger amounts, by certain types of bacteria that infect beer.

Lager. Beer that is fermented cool using lager yeast (*Saccharomyces carlsbergensis*) and stored cold for a period of weeks in order to give it a clean, smooth flavor. From the German verb meaning "to store."

Lauter tun. A vessel with a perforated false bottom, used to strain the sweet wort off the spent grains after mashing.

Lovibond. The scale, in degrees, on which American brewers measure the color of malt and beer.

Malt. Barley or other grain which has been soaked, allowed to sprout, and then dried. Sprouting allows development of the enzymes that bring about starch conversion in the mash.

Malt extract. Syrup or powder made by removing water from sweet wort.

Mash. 1. (verb) To make a thick mixture of hot water with crushed malt and, in some cases, adjuncts, in which the grain starches are converted to sugar. 2. (noun) The mixture described above.

Mouthfeel. The sensation of fullness in the mouth, created by dextrins and proteins in the beer.

Noble hops. Hops of relatively low alpha acid content but with fine aromatic and flavoring properties. May be used for bittering as well as finishing.

Original gravity. The specific gravity of the wort before fermentation begins.

Oxidation. Any chemical reaction involving oxygen. Oxidation gives beer an unpleasant taste.

Pale malt. Ordinary barley malt, dried at low temperatures to minimize color.

Pitch. To add brewer's yeast to wort.

Polyclar. A clarifying agent. Also known as PVP.

Priming. Adding sugar to beer before bottling.

Protein. Any complex organic compound containing nitrogen.

Rack. To transfer beer from one vessel to another, leaving the sediment behind.

Real ale. Draft ale that is naturally conditioned in the cask and dispensed without using an external source of pressure.

Recirculate. To pour the cloudy runoff through the grain bed in the lauter tun, in order to filter it.

Rehydrate. To add dried yeast to warm water, so that the yeast cells can absorb the water and be reactivated prior to pitching.

Runoff. The sweet wort that is drained from the lauter tun and recirculated prior to sparging.

Sanitize. To make clean and essentially free of microorganisms.

Silica gel. A clarifying agent.

Slurry. A thick, opaque suspension of yeast cells or other particles.

Sparge. To rinse the grain bed in the lauter tun with hot water, in order to recover the residual sugar.

Specialty malt. Malt prepared by any of several processes which develops a strong flavor, dark color, or other desired properties.

Specific gravity. A measure of density; in other words, how heavy a given volume of liquid is, when compared with pure water. Malt sugar increases the specific gravity of wort, and fermentation (by removing the sugar) lowers it.

Starter culture. A small volume of sterile wort which is inoculated with brewer's yeast so that the yeast will grow to a sufficient quantity for pitching.

Sterile. Totally devoid of living organisms.

Strain. Yeast (often grown from a single cell) which shares a common genetic makeup and specific traits, such as alcohol tolerance and flavoring properties.

Sugar. Any of a number of simple carbohydrates with a sweet taste, which are fermentable by yeast and other organisms.

Terminal gravity. The specific gravity of beer after fermentation is completed. Also called *final gravity* and *present gravity*.

Top-fermenting. Describes yeast that flocculates relatively early in the fermentation and is carried up into the kraeusen by carbon dioxide bubbles.

Total alkalinity. The bicarbonate ion content of a water sample. It is important in brewing because high total alkalinity, unless corrected, will interfere with conversion.

Trub. The break material that drops to the bottom of the boil kettle, settling tank, and fermenter.

Wild yeast. Any yeast that is introduced accidentally into wort or beer from the environment. Many kinds of wild yeasts produce off-flavors in beer.

Wort. A sugar solution derived from grain by mashing and sparging.

Yeast. A relatively large, complex, single-celled microorganism. It thrives on sugar, which it ferments, but also requires oxygen and other nutrients for growth.

BIBLIOGRAPHY

Beer and Brewing. Boulder, Colorado: Brewers Publications. Transcripts of the talks given at the annual conference of the American Homebrewers Association. Specific references are cited below, but the series is very worthwhile. A new volume is published each year.

zymurgy. Boulder, Colorado: The American Homebrewers Association. This journal is published each season, with a special issue coming out late in the fall devoted to a special topic. Specific references are cited below. Back issues are available. A one-year subscription, which includes membership in the AHA, costs $25. Write to: AHA, P.O. Box 1679, Boulder, CO 80306-1679.

Beer and Beer Styles

The Beer Styles Series. Boulder, Colorado: Brewers Publications. An ongoing project that will eventually comprise 15 volumes, one on each of the world's great beer styles. So far, three numbers have appeared: *Pale Ale,* by Dr. Terry Foster, 1990; *Continental Pilsener,* by Dave Miller, 1990; and *Lambic,* by Jean-Xavier Guinard, 1991.

Eckhardt, Fred. *The Essentials of Beer Style.* Portland, Oregon: Fred Eckhardt Associates, 1989.

Jackson, Michael. *The 1991 Simon and Schuster Pocket Guide to Beer.* New York: Simon and Schuster, 1991.

————. *The New World Guide to Beer.* Philadelphia: The Running Press, 1988.

Extract Brewing

Burch, Byron. *Brewing Quality Beers.* Fulton, California: Joby Books, 1986. Clear, concise, accurate information.

Papazian, Charlie. *The Complete Joy of Brewing.* New York: Avon Books, 1983.

Grain Brewing

Downer, Ron. "Essentials of Step-Infusion Mashing." *Beer and Brewing,* vol. 10 (1990), pp. 107–29.

Line, Dave. *The Big Book of Brewing.* Andover, Hampshire, U.K.: Amateur Winemaker, 1974. Focuses on British ales.

Miller, Dave. *The Complete Handbook of Home Brewing.* Pownal, Vermont: Garden Way Publishing, 1988.

————. "Issues in All-Grain Brewing." *Beer and Brewing*, vol. 8 (1988), pp. 43–69.

Noonan, Greg. *Brewing Lager Beer*. Boulder, Colorado: Brewers Publications, 1986. Focuses on the decoction method of mashing. Excellent for the technically minded.

zymurgy Special Grain Brewing Issue (1985).

Fermentation

Fix, George. "Yeast." *Beer and Brewing*, vol. 7 (1987), pp. 153–70. Focuses on flavor traits of specific yeast strains.

————. "Yeast Cycles." *zymurgy Special Grain Brewing Issue* (1985). Overview of the biochemistry of yeast.

zymurgy Special Yeast Issue (1989). Many excellent articles. Byron Burch's (on yeast strains) is especially informative.

Brewing Science

Fix, George. *Principles of Brewing Science*. Boulder, Colorado: Brewers Publications, 1989. Essential advanced text.

zymurgy Special Troubleshooting Issue (1987). Information on off-flavors and how to avoid them.

Hops

Fix, George. "Hop Flavor in Beer." *Beer and Brewing*, vol. 8 (1988),

pp. 183–99.

Wills, Dave. "Hop Madness." *Beer and Brewing*, vol. 9 (1989), pp. 175–91.

zymurgy Special Hops Issue (1989).

Recipe Formulation

Burch, Byron. "Recipe Formulation." *Beer and Brewing*, vol. 7 (1987), pp. 21–37.

Carey, Dan. "Brewing a Maibock." *Beer and Brewing*, vol. 8 (1988), pp. 201–19.

Miller, Dave. "Experimenting with Munich Malt." *Beer and Brewing*, vol. 10 (1990), pp. 77–84.

Mosher, Randy. "The Flavorful World of Malt." *Beer and Brewing*, vol. 10 (1990), pp. 55–76.

Draft Beer Systems

Burch, Byron. "A Great System for Draft Beers." *Beer and Brewing*, vol. 10 (1990), pp. 177–89. Also discusses filtration and counter-pressure bottling.

Rager, Jackie. "Soda Keg Draft Systems." *zymurgy*, vol. 12, no. 5 (Winter 1989), pp. 24–25.

Filtration and Counterpressure Bottling

Daniel, Steve. "How to Build a Simple Counter-pressure Bottle Filler." *zymurgy*, vol. 13, no. 1 (Spring 1990), pp. 36–38.

Hanson, Todd. "Home Filtration and Carbonation." *Beer and*

Brewing, vol. 7 (1987), pp. 93–117.

Morris, Rodney. "Beer Filtration for the Homebrewer." *zymurgy*, vol. 13, no. 2 (Summer 1990), pp. 33–37.

Large-Batch Brewing

Burch, Byron. "The Beer Essentials." *Beer and Brewing*, vol. 9 (1989), pp. 101–12. Describes the author's tower-style 10-gallon home brewery.

Downer, Ron. "Essentials of Step-Infusion Mashing." *Beer and Brewing*, vol. 10 (1990), pp. 107–30. Includes a description of the author's brewery and plans for building a lauter tun out of a picnic cooler.

Olchowski, Charlie. "Innovations in Brewing Equipment." *Beer and Brewing*, vol. 7 (1987), pp. 219–33.

SOURCES FOR EQUIPMENT AND INGREDIENTS

My publisher tells me that the number one response to my earlier book, *The Complete Handbook of Home Brewing*, has been, "Where do I get these things?" Therefore, I am including some advice on ways to track down the special equipment and brewing ingredients that you will need.

If you don't know anyone involved in home brewing, the first place to check is your local yellow pages, which probably has a listing under "Brewing Supplies" or "Wine-making Supplies." Your local shop is the place you should deal with first. They have the most to gain by serving you well, and they are also the people you are in the best position to evaluate. Even if they do not carry what you need, they may be able to special-order it.

A second source of good information is your local homebrewing club. Most metropolitan areas now have one or more. These experienced homebrewers will be glad to share their experiences, positive and negative, with different suppliers. One way to find out about a local club is through your local supplier. In addition, the American Homebrewers Association has a list of all the clubs in the country that are registered with them (and by the way, club members, if your club is not registered with the AHA, it should be!), and they will gladly tell you if there is a registered club in your area. Their phone number is 303-447-0816. They also have a FAX number, 303-447-2825. Their address is given in the Bibliography under the heading of their magazine, *zymurgy*.

Speaking of which, the advertisements in *zymurgy* are an excellent source of information on firms that specialize in selling supplies by mail-order. There are many reasons to become a member of the AHA, the ads in their periodical being one. Often, suppliers specialize in a particular area (for example, grain brewing or large-batch equipment), and their ads will mention this, which will help you find a source for the particular item you want.

Finally, you can turn to the Home Wine and Beer Trade Association, a group whose name is self-explanatory. The Executive Secretary of the Association, Dee Roberson, maintains a database listing of all affiliated dealers. She can provide you with the names, addresses, and phone numbers of suppliers in your area, including the name of a knowledgeable salesperson who will be happy to discuss your needs. Send a self-addressed, stamped envelope to:

Dee Roberson, Executive Secretary
Home Wine and Beer Trade Association
604 North Miller Road
Valrico, Florida 33594

Ms. Roberson is also available by telephone (813-685-4261) or FAX (813-681-5625).

To summarize, here are my recommendations for tracking down suppliers:

■ First, check your yellow pages to see if there is a home wine and beer supplier in your area. If so, try them out.

■ Second, find out if there is a nearby club. If so, join it.

■ Third, look through the ads in *zymurgy*.

■ Fourth, contact the HWBTA.

One point to keep in mind when shopping by mail is that malt and malt extract are very heavy. Shipping costs can comprise a large part of the total bill. That is why a local supplier may be cheaper, even if their prices are not as low as those of a mail-order firm.

INDEX

(Illustrations are indicated by page numbers in *italics*; charts and tables are indicated by page numbers in **bold**.)